Identity

IDENTITY

Vernon White

scm press

British Library Cataloguing in Publication data

A catalogue record for this book is available
from the British Library

0 334 02890 6

First published in 2002 by SCM Press
9-17 St Albans Place, London N1 0NX

www.scm-canterburypress.co.uk

SCM Press is a division of
SCM-Canterbury Press Ltd

Printed and bound in Great Britain by
Bookmarque, Croydon

CONTENTS

PREFACE

Society and *church*?

Why is there any need to commission books on society and church? Is there anything really to discuss? That suspicious question may be asked from at least two quite distinct perspectives. On the one hand, most people in our highly secularized society will regard church as, at most, an institution of voluntary association (like the Royal Society for the Protection of Birds or a cycling association), attracting like-minded people. It may (or may not) be thought a good thing (for other people, who are into that sort of thing). Church is unlikely, however, to be considered essential to the fabric or self-understanding of society as a whole, even by those who admit Christianity's historically significant role in the self-understanding and development of our society and polity. Entirely marginal to society, like the RSPB and cycling groups, it may allowably engage with wider society in order to pursue its special interest agenda (protection of birds, provision of cycle lanes). But it would have to do so by arguing and campaigning on commonly agreed ground, not by appeal to some special sense of society and social good.

On the other hand, those within churches might feel there is little point in asking whether and how church relates to society, since it is manifestly obvious that, empirically, it just does. Simply as a social institution existing within society, the Church is, necessarily and unavoidably, actively engaged in it theologically, spiritually and educationally, whilst, as an institution, it has had to respond to its changing context. At one level, this is an empirical statement, yet it is one that will often receive a theological expression and interpretation. Social engagement is often seen, not as an incidental, accidental or peripheral matter – what the Church *does* – but as aspects of its central self-definition – what the Church *is*. The Church's institutional engagement in education, welfare, government, and so on, may be seen in terms of the Church's self-defining mission, or as part of its self-understanding. The ways in which the Church is engaged in society reflects a long history in which, at its best, the Church has held a dynamic and historical vision of its task and existence, grounded in the mystery of the trinitarian God. (In the last century the Church has abandoned a static view of ministry, and no longer sees itself as given its final form by Christ at its origin. Theologians and church members respond in many changing ways to the world around it.) The Church as an institution adapts to its changing circumstances, whilst also pronouncing on matters of societal concern within those areas historically within its remit.

Yet such a confident note belies the crisis which afflicts the very existence of the Church in British society. In the last fifty years culture has become almost completely secularized in its public sphere. The language of God, once quite common in public life in the first half of the twentieth century, and for centuries before that, is now muted, if not almost silent. The occasional politician refers to God in a half embarrassed way, or religion is seen as dangerous, irrational and the cause of wars and terrorism. The Church and God-talk are marginalized. Moreover, where the Church does engage with society, on issues of social and political concern, it also finds difficulty in seeing the possibility and significance of God-talk. The Church tends to adopt secular modes of discernment and secular criteria in its reports and contributions to debate. In this situation it is far from clear how the rapid changes inside the churches in the last fifty years relate at all to the indifference of the world. How may the Churches make any contribution to British society?

Asking this question is the task of this series. The purpose of

Society and Church is to ask how the Churches can claim public space, as *Christian* Churches, in a legitimate and effective way in a society that has become as secular as British society now is. The question will be answered in a way that engages with three overlapping, but distinct audiences. First, there will be church people who care about the future of the Church and of society. Second, there are those who might be called the half-believer. They will read religious articles in the press, or will listen to religious programmes on radio and television, but are unlikely to enter a church building except occasionally: they believe and doubt (or believe but fail to find the relevance and significance of God – or at least the Church) at the same time. Thirdly, there are those suspicious of the Church, or not terribly interested in religion, but who are committed to the topic and will read the book for the sake of the subject.

The series will address the central issue of the marginalization of the Church by commissioning books on specific topics, written in a concrete way that avoids abstraction. On this issue, is there anything which is illuminated by referring to a theological standpoint, within the specific historical, cultural, political and ecclesiastical dynamics of the situation? The purpose of this approach is to see how the distinctiveness of what is modelled in one work may illuminate another quite different situation. 'I had not thought that you could look at it in this way.' The series will not favour one particular way of reading the situation, nor hold a particular theological or political viewpoint. We shall commission from both left and right (whatever those terms might mean in our postmodern world), but we will always emphasize that the relationship of church and society has changed so much in the new millennium that conventional religious and theological strategies are no longer appropriate.

It is clear that this analysis is not shared widely inside the churches. There is, rather, a sense of complacency about the present and future status and contribution of the Church to national life in Britain. Equally there is no clear understanding among the Churches of what their relationship to society might be, or how it might effectively be defended. Theologically there is grave doubt as to whether public theology is possible any more. A public theology has theological integrity in addressing society, while being responsible to the issues in society. In church terms, it means that the idea of being 'a church for society' is deeply problematic.

Those who write in this series take this crisis with the utmost seriousness. They believe that the Church still has something to offer society, and believe that it is part of its very rationale that it should do so, but they understand all too well the difficulties of the present time. The series will take into account the massive changes which have occurred in British society and politics since 1945, and authors will refer to these developments in their particular work. But the series is not an exercise in contemporary history. Its aim is to initiate a conversation about whether public theology is any longer possible. Have the Churches anything to say which it is worth the world listening to? That is the stark question addressed by this series.

Vernon White examines human identity in the crisis of modernity. On his reading, the immense changes in family life and paid employment over recent decades have rendered problematic the making of personal commitments, the bearing of responsibilities and the living out of roles. His concern is therefore with the nature of faithfulness and loyalty, which he discusses philosophically as well as theologically. The overarching question here is the nature of "being a person", and whether personhood is still a defensible concept. The argument in defence of a unified view of being a person over time, with all the issues of faithfulness which this raises, draws heavily on biblical, theological and philosophical accounts of human nature in relationship to God. The clarity and precision of the writing develop a justification for seeing identity in relationships as the central feature of modern life. The book makes an admirable contribution to *Society and Church* by showing how the means to sustain a fulfilling life are provided from the Jewish and Christian traditions.

INTRODUCTION

IDENTITY, CHANGE AND FAITHFULNESS: A THEOLOGICAL TASK

The argument of this book is straightforward. The rapid pace of change is straining our sense of identity, often to breaking point. Christian theology has unique resources to confront this. In particular it offers the neglected notion of *faithfulness*. So the plea at the heart of this book is simply this: we need to rediscover faithfulness. It is a vital way of living with integrity through change.

A little more to introduce these issues. First, the experience of change, because it is so pervasive. Change shapes us individually and corporately, biologically and socially. It is a constituent of the physical universe, a defining feature in most construals of matter, space, time. In some sense it may be a constituent of God. The range, radicality, pace and meaning of change may vary, but our experience of it remains – even when notions of an ultimate changelessness are invoked by metaphysicians. It is a particularly powerful experience. Even a commonplace experience of change, like watching a child grow up or the seasons pass, is remarkable. Above all it is ambivalent and disturbing. 'Wonder and sadness is the lot of change', says the poet, speaking for us all.[1] It is not hard to see why. Change, inseparable from time, touches on raw spots of our being. It affects our *identity*, and does so paradoxically. On the one hand it resonates with hope, creativity, new life, the resolution of wrong. On the other hand it reminds us of risk, loss, irrevocability, mortality. If change moves us on to something new, what happens to the old? We leave something which was (for all its faults) at least a known part of us. We face something which will (for all its possibilities) become an unknown part of us. It might end us altogether. Change will eventually bring physical death and, even before that, delivers another kind of death by the question it puts to our very sense of self. For the 'we' who will change seems insecure. If we are only the sum total of our past experiences, do we remain at all when these are supplanted by new experiences? If we are someone yet to be, will we be so radically changed that it makes little sense to talk of the same person?

Social change carries this sense of ambivalence and disturbance just as profoundly as natural and biological change. This is inevitable when we are so substantially formed out of our social roles and relationships. It means there will always be new or revisionist histories to be written about major social events like the rise and fall of empires, the enclosure of land, industrial revolution. Because such change brings profound consequences at every level of social and personal being it makes adequate description, let alone evaluation, a long, difficult, tentative task. New perspectives are bound to emerge and re-emerge. The moral goods and ills of major social change will always resist easy, naive, or reductive treatment. They are the social expression of the existential wonder and sadness in the poet's soul.

Our current context forces the issue on us now with particular intensity. Change is rampant, and its consequences for identity felt more keenly than before. There are major, rapid and interconnected changes in information technology, globalization, work and employment practices, consumerism, family structures, all of which affect us deeply, ambivalently, and at every level. A particular feature of this current experience of change is that it has no clear direction. It is a symptom of deep-seated confusion, often identified as a legacy of the failed Enlightenment 'project'. This has left us in a situation where no overarching traditions or metanarratives hold sway to regulate or interpret change. Christian faith and rationalism have both suffered deconstruction, in principle and practice. They have not been able to sustain ways of thinking and living which command consensus and give coherence. At both personal and social levels this has left us with the sense of moving constantly from one epoch to another: worse, from one epoch to no discernible epoch at all. The ensuing ideological and social vacuum has filled with competing, transient meanings and practices. It is a loose and unstable coalition, held together only by the drive of consumerism in a global market and the managerial–technological efficiency of instrumental reason (i.e. the necessary conditions for getting anything done at all).

All this has serious consequences for society generally: but again, it also has consequences specifically for the self and our sense of identity. With the demise of overarching traditions we can, temporarily, conceive our*selves* with some confidence: we are liberated from authority and empowered by reason to create our own destiny. But the onslaught on reason and social distintegration quickly erodes this confidence. We are now just 'sites' of varying performance and passing roles. Whether these are imposed by social constraints, our own subconscious drives, or self-created, it is a kind of selfhood which disintegrates easily.[2] The evidence most often cited in individual terms is the high rates of stress, depression and mental illness. In social terms there is the breakdown of established long-term relationships in family and community life. This represents a very profound disturbance. It intensifies our general experience of change with the further bewilderment of instability and unpredictability. It is a self-reinforcing cycle, because the disintegrating effect of change merely drives us to further change.

True, the sense of instability can be exaggerated. It is a recurring vanity of every age to think it is suffering radically new experiences. Frank Kermode reminds us of this when he describes our social condition in the terms of the social decay of the late nineteenth century.[3] There is also no reason to think social or personal change should be linear and predictable, nor that we can ever tame it with some rational theory of change.

In this sense every age may find itself caught by surprise. Moreover, it is important to retain the positive perspective of change, even at its current level of intensity and unpredictability. As old social and personal identities crumble, old oppressions are unmasked and new vitality and creativity is released (who would deny, for example, the value of some new developments in education?). Nonetheless, the general point stands. It is not much disputed that current levels of change have brought disintegration and disorientation. Identity has been profoundly affected, for better or for worse. That is what change does.

It is also not likely to be disputed that we have coped poorly with these levels of change. That is the case whether or not they are deemed exceptional, and however they are evaluated. This judgement that we have not coped particularly well arises out of recent history. In spite of the huge benefits of change, we have also been saturated by the suffering brought in its wake. One obvious reason is that the sheer pace of scientific and technological advance and economic globalization has outstripped our moral maturity to deal with the changes they bring. As indicated already, the absence of adequate moral or religious systems has left instrumental reason to fill the gap – and when this is combined with the unfettered release of atavistic fears, prejudices, self-preoccupations, the consequence has been inevitable: the availability of efficient technical means has quickly been turned to ends of destruction, manipulation, instant self-gratification, whenever there is threat, stress, or sheer greed. Ethnic and religious conflict, the relentless drive to genetic control, the enslavement of a whole generation within a consumer identity, family breakdown and widespread depression are some of the most obvious manifestations. Again, we might want to say that such grit in the process of change is neither fundamentally new nor entirely avoidable. We might even want to take reassurance from some sort of long-term evolutionary perspective: we can hope that the necessary socio-biological adaptations to change may occur in due course. Or we might look for some renewed moral maturity, a new metanarrative derived from interreligious dialogue or some other global coalition. But none of this deals decisively with our current situation. It remains the case that we have not coped well and do not *yet* seem to have the resources to do any better.

How then can we best live through this process of change? It is here that the question and answer cries out for theology and its resources. Is there anything about *God* – the God of Judaeo-Christian faith – which illuminates change? In particular, does this faith propose a way of living with the effects of change on personal identity? I can offer no new sociological or philosophical analysis about the situation, nor any new theory of change, but I do want to bring this theological question to bear at every point of the argument.

For much of the northern world this may seem wilfully oblique, even perverse. Why appeal to a contested, remote, abstract, even fictitious reality, in order to cope with an immediate and incontrovertible experience? The response is this. The 'God of Judaeo-Christian faith' means much more than a remote and abstract reality. He/she is revealed through a long, rich, history of engagement with real experience and reflection, itself spanning vast social and cultural change, from pre-modern desert life to postmodern urban life. The pivotal points of this revelation have transformed the experience of women and men across all this huge variety of history and geography. As a matter of human record this cannot be written off as an abstraction. And if it is thought to be fictitious – the projection of a reality rather than a revelation – there is always the invitation to suppose it *might* be true. This is not an unreasonable request: namely, to suspend outright disbelief just long enough to enter imaginatively the light it claims to shed. It makes sense to suspend disbelief a little in order to enter a little further, to see where it leads.

Another response is simply this: Why not? Why not quarry again these rich seams of historic theistic faith? Why not try this again when no serious alternative is succeeding? It is evident that theology has become a largely forgotten resource. There may still be a good deal of generalized spirituality (rather than straightforward secularization) in late-modernity, but disciplined theological thinking and living have certainly been in decline. The same is true for other historic traditions and metanarratives, discarded in the name of liberation. It all means that we have been negotiating the rapidly increasing change of recent decades with rapidly decreasing theological convictions – yet still we don't seem to have negotiated it particularly well. Rehabilitating theology in some way thus becomes once more a real option.

A further reason arises from internal developments in Christian faith and theology. Theology is increasingly attuned to the presence of God in change and complexity, rather than simply in static social realities.[4] It has also become more ready to accept change in God (to supplement, if not supplant, classical notions of divine changelessness). These developments suggest that doctrines of God may have more light to shed in a context of acute change – and we would do well to revisit their resources for dealing with it.

The suggestion that a theological tradition may have an answer to offer does not imply an easy answer, nor a unique one, nor one that applies univocally across the diversity of this changing world. That is not the point at all. It may itself have fluidity and flexibility, and it may resonate with other attempts to navigate change. Theology is not necessarily at odds with all forms of plurality. On the other hand, to the extent that theology does go beyond plurality and imply some transcendence and universality, that must not count against it. Radical postmodernism which relativizes and atomizes all 'truth' itself needs to be challenged. It is intrinsically implausible. It has nothing to offer, and nothing to connect us. Any truth claim which operates effectively within this changing world cannot be wholly trapped in just one part of it. So some sort of transcendence *is* required. Some sort of universality *is* necessary. Something enduring must exist for anything to exist. And that is just what a truly theological perspective on change can include without embarrassment. It must and can marry change and transcendence – and that will be its strength, not its weakness.

The specific theological 'answer' of faithfulness that I am

proposing clearly incorporates all this. It will not mean anything merely static, merely conservative, merely ancient or merely (post)modern. It will be a notion of faithfulness which itself involves time and change. Equally, it will imply an enduring insight which will always, and in every situation, have some fresh light to shed. Its meaning will derive ultimately from the meaning of God himself. It will matter for all human life. As such it is something like an 'icon', as Rowan Williams uses the term.[5] It is an insight into one of the most basic conditions for living any common life successfully and, better still, *truthfully*. It is not just about finding a useful social convention, nor even a compelling ideal. It is about an essential and God-given dimension of all true human being without which we cease to be truly human. 'Faithfulness', as a key constituent of maintaining human identity within the process of change, is just such an icon – and as with Williams' icons (childhood, charity, remorse) it must not be lost. This why this book pivots round faithfulness. It proves a compelling answer to the question that theology puts to change. It is something which needs to be re-formed and rediscovered as much as theology itself.

The structure of the discussion which follows reflects all these concerns. Because it claims widespread significance for faithfulness it must begin with some trawl of social philosophy and a good deal more historical and recent theology. Only then will it turn to specific social practices and more practically based issues of contemporary life and society. In this way its meaning is established in a wider context as well as in current experience. As a method this does not always win easy assent. There is a natural impatience to derive meaning first from present experience and practices. But that privileges the immediacy of current experience too much. Instead there must be a real dialogue between past and present, general and local, abstract and concrete. This will front-load the book with a certain amount of abstract discussion, but the main point should still emerge clearly enough. Change calls for new forms of faithfulness – and theology has something very important to say on its behalf.

1

FAITHFULNESS AND LOYALTY: SOME RECENT COMPASS POINTS

The significance of faithfulness as an essential moral good in a modern society has been hailed before. Nearly 100 years ago the American idealist philosopher Josiah Royce expressed it through the concept of loyalty.[1] The position he took is well worth outlining. It provides a useful point of reference in social philosophy and a connection with some recent theology. Not least, it offers some provisional definitions of the notion in the context of a society bearing at least some of the hallmarks of our later modern/postmodern situation. It was a society in which the relation of individual to community was becoming increasingly problematic. Royce characterized it as 'expanding, complexifying, socially plural' and 'increasingly mechanical' as distinct from organic: that is, a context in which individuals function more like cogs in a machine than as members of a body who willingly identifying themselves with the whole. It was a society 'riven by inner conflict' and the sheer 'multitude of passing events' which obscured any sense of overall unity and purpose. The effect on individuals was alienating. They 'cannot always recall the sense in which they identify their own lives with what has been or with what is yet to come'.[2] 'Loyalty' was Royce's response to this situation – worked out in greatest detail in *The Philosophy of Loyalty* and maintained throughout his later works.

Royce preferred the term 'loyalty' to either fidelity or faith-fulness. He defined the latter simply as persistence in a cause or relationship. By loyalty he also meant our initial and willing acceptance of the cause. His summary definition of loyalty was 'the willing and practical and thoroughgoing devotion of a person to a cause'. The ultimate cause was specified as loyalty to loyalty itself, in order to provide a conceptual and practical tool to distinguish worthy causes and arbitrate between conflicting causes (i.e. the cause to be preferred is always the cause which most promotes loyalty). In his later work 'community' replaced 'cause' as the object of loyalty, analysed through commonality of custom, language, religion. But there was no significant retraction of the central thesis about loyalty itself.

The Philosophy of Loyalty is a systematic work, claiming much for its subject. Loyalty is a supreme good and the fulfil-ment of the whole moral law: 'all . . . fundamental duties of the civilized man . . . are instances of loyalty to loyalty'.[3] As such it is a core concept in an overall metaphysic. The supreme ethi-cal value of loyalty is taken as something 'essentially good' and 'true', not just pragmatically successful, and as something which relates to 'a real unity with all experience'.[4] This meta-physical framework implies a refinement of the definition which is eventually made explicit. Strictly speaking, 'loyalty to loyalty' cannot after all be the ultimate good or ultimate claim on us. Instead it must be that reality which makes loyalty *true*. This reality must be the ultimate (if mysterious) 'master of life'- which is a metaphysical or spiritual mystery. This resonates readily with religious language. It recalls the words of the biblical parable of the talents which tells of the master who has gone into a far country, leaving the servants to be loyal in his cause. Royce also states explicitly that 'loyalty is the will to believe in something eternal and to express that belief in the practical life of a human being. . . . Religion is the interpretation both of the eternal . . . and of the spirit of loyalty'.[5] His final words are specifically scriptural: 'Lo I am with you always, even unto the end of the world.' Royce is talking about religion ('an expression of emotion and imagination') rather than the discipline of theology, but clearly the theological question is being raised. A theological meta-physic is being signalled, even if it is not developed.

Royce offers much more on the practical nature of loyalty. It is never mere emotion, but always entails action in the service of the cause. Crucially, this attitude and action of loyalty (to any cause) unifies the life of the individual, giving it 'centre, fixity, stability'.[6] It furnishes a unifying purposes and thereby 'makes of us conscious and unified moral persons', rather than just 'a cauldron of seething and bubbling efforts'.[7] However, this does not mean that loyalty is merely the exercise of uni-formity or routine in carrying out purposes. In particular circumstances 'loyalty is perfectly consistent with originality. The loyal man may often have to show his loyalty by some act which no mere routine predetermines. He may have to be inventive of his duties as he is faithful to them.'[8]

As for the cause itself, it is never wholly impersonal but involves other people in relationships. Loyalty therefore binds the individual to the wider community in a way which fulfils individuality (or selfhood). This happens in the very act of submitting to the larger cause or community because it is a *willing* submission or self-identification with the cause. This unites the exercise of personal autonomy with the authority of a social morality which transcends the individual. It distin-guishes itself from 'mere social conformity' or 'mere bondage to tradition' because 'what has made loyalty a good has never been the convention which undertook to enforce it, but has always been the spiritual dignity which lies in being loyal'.[9] As such, loyalty can be a critical notion. It can test the worth of any cause, cope with competing causes, and unify disparate given causes such as family, community, state. As indicated, it does this by the overriding principle of loyalty to loyalty itself – which demands a maximizing of loyalty in any choices or priorities which have to be made. This means that while loyalty demands decisiveness in the choice of a cause and fidelity in pursuing it, loyalty itself could also require a partic-ular cause to be revoked (e.g. in the light of new knowledge about its true nature or consequences).

Royce acknowledges there are natural parameters to possible or likely objects of our loyalty. Broadly speaking we are most likely to serve 'such causes as [our] natural temperament and social opportunity suggest' – though such a natural field of loyalty may always be deliberately extended in the greater cause of loyalty to loyalty.[10] He suggests that no single individual can be the sole object of loyalty because loyalty is always a matter of wider relations or 'ties'. Family ties belong to this natural field. Larger social–political organizations are also proper objects of loyalty, in principle, but he acknowledges the difficulty pinpointed by Hegel: the 'self-estranged spirit' of modernity will not easily identify with much wider organization. His solution here is not so very different from a good deal of recent communitarian thinking. Smaller-scale forms of civil life and community are to be valued and reinvigorated: loyalty is to be essayed first in relation to the local and provincial.[11] This then provides the training ground for larger loyalties to the nation, or even beyond. Through the customs, symbols, ceremonies of limited and local organizations we are furnished with the imagination and vision necessary to sustain allegiance to broader social goals.

This notion of training in the practice of loyalty is a further reminder that Royce deals with loyalty at both the practical and ideal levels. Loyalty is a form of moral action which has to be sustained in a difficult world, through disappointment, setback and counter pressures. Its truest meaning only emerges, therefore, by practising it in such a world: 'strain, endurance, sacrifice, toil . . . teach us what loyalty is'.[12] Strong leaders are identified as part of the practical means to achieve this. But that is not enough. The 'idealization' of a cause is also necessary to learn and sustain loyalty. Religion in particular has a function in this process, by 'linking our causes . . . to a world which seems to us to be superhuman'.[13] Thus idealism in both the popular and philosophical sense informs the meaning of loyalty at the very point where the discussion is most practical. This idealism also explains the robust universalism of Royce's proposal. Loyalty, however hard to achieve, is uncompromisingly a good for all, because it can always be the goal for all. There is a Kantian view of the moral life at work here. We pursue an absolute and categoric ideal which gives meaning by its pursuit in time, even though its fulfilment lies in a completion beyond any one moment in time.[14]

In spite of this thorough and systematic treatment, Royce's proposal has not had much influence. He has stood 'virtually alone in raising these questions about loyalty, philosophically'.[15] There are some obvious reasons to account for this. Generally speaking, Royce's underlying philosophical idealism has found it hard to survive more recent intellectual trends. Specifically, he may have overstated his case by claiming it as a supreme good from which *all* other goods, rights and duties can be deduced. The extent to which the formal principle of 'loyalty to loyalty' provides a practical criterion for distinguishing the relative worth of causes is also arguable.[16] The sheer scale of tragically misplaced loyalties in the ensuing century sharpens this point. The ethnic, nationalistic and ideological loyalties of Nazism, Stalinism, African and Balkan conflicts, have proved too powerful to be checked and chastened by a formal principle. The fanatical attack on the USA which has heralded the twenty-first century makes the same point.

But some have been influenced. Gabriel Marcel (preferring 'fidelity') has acknowledged a debt to Royce. He has reflected at some length on the notions of both commitment and loyalty. By pursuing them through more existentialist categories he has added new substance to some of Royce's definitions.

Marcel begins from the question of how he can 'think' his own life at all, and especially how he can reliably think of it in relation to the future. If I do not know or control the future, how can I promise anything? 'How can I promise – commit my future?' [17] Yet we do still make promises and commitments – which implies we can think our future even if we cannot entirely control it. In other words, we can distinguish ourselves from the experience of momentary situations and can conceive ourselves existing through a whole life-process. In this way the commitment of a promise implies a being who transcends any one moment of time, and an act of commitment is an act of this transcendent self. Fidelity to this commitment therefore entails fidelity to this transcendent self as much as a response to the 'cause' or object of the commitment. In this sense there is a real personal 'presence' in commitment – and I let down my own transcendent being if I repudiate it. This further means that any change in either myself as subject or in the other as the object of the commitment will not justify repudiating a promise. This is because I have already committed my transcendent self (i.e. the whole of myself), not just my momentary self.[18] Only insincerity at the point of commitment, or the rash promise of a drunkard, will release us – but only because it was never a real commitment of the whole self in the first place. This mounts a case for a very 'strong' view of fidelity.

The motive for fidelity, however, is not simply to be self-consistent through time for the sake of our own integrity. That is just pride! It arises out of a profound relationship and response to the other, as well as to myself. It has to do with the 'direct and unchallengeable experience' of encountering a 'thou'. This 'thou' may also be a wider cause, as long as this is conceived as 'supra-personal' rather than a merely non-personal, formal or abstract principle. It is here that Marcel engages explicitly with Royce. He also echoes Royce in his insistence that this fidelity is no passive 'inertia' of the soul, but 'creative' in its response to the presence of the self and other in this relationship. Ultimately this sense of a dynamic and transcendent 'presence' in the relationship of commitment is taken even further. It has to do with God. When we take the risk of unconditional commitment, we find ourselves in a state of being which participates in Being itself. The ultimate act of commitment is 'an act of transcendence having its ontological counterpart in the hold God has over me'.[19]

There is no systematic advocacy of fidelity here. Marcel is exploring aspects of the phenomenology of human existence rather than proposing a major philosophical or political programme. But it is one of the few recent philosophical appropriations of the notion to suggest its significance and fruitfulness. And it is notable how this readily echoes some of

Royce's major themes, in spite of their philosophical differences. The fidelity of promise and commitment is a substantive fulfilment of human identity through time and change. It is a dynamic notion to do with personal or supra-personal social relationships, not just a purely formal principle. Most significant of all, it entails notions of transcendence. It provokes or presupposes questions of metaphysics. It presses the question of God. As noted, Royce had begun to set out a theological agenda in his concluding sections. Marcel reinforces this need. The theological dimension is hard to avoid.

So what of theology itself? How has it dealt with Royce and his agenda? The response has been surprisingly slight. But some have seen its importance. H. Richard Niebuhr, for instance, reorientates the issue theologically in an entirely straightforward way.[20] *God* is the ultimate source and centre of value, so it is God who is identified explicitly as the ultimate object of loyalty. Equally, because God is the principle of all being and source of all selves, all beings themselves have value and command loyalty: God gives value and demands loyalty to all things, not just to himself. Radical monotheism (as Niebuhr calls it) therefore entails universal loyalty, as distinct from merely tribal or competitive loyalties. This resonates with Royce's ultimate principle of 'loyalty to loyalty', but replaces it explicitly with its theistic basis: the ultimate principle is better understood as loyalty to God in all things. 'Such universal loyalty cannot be loyalty to loyalty, as Royce would have it, but is loyalty to all existents as bound together by a loyalty that is not only resident in them but transcends them.'[21]

Niebuhr's treatment of ethical and anthropological implications also follows Royce (and Marcel) closely. There is the same insistence that loyalty and its promises of commitment fulfil human identity. It gives purpose, substance, and unity to a life lived in the world and through time. The self is only properly itself when it is involved in commitments.

Loyalty or faithfulness values the center . . . and makes that center its cause for which to live and labor. In this active faith the loyal self organizes its activities and seeks to organize its world. [It] . . . expresses itself in a *sacramentum*, an oath of fealty, a vow of commitment.[22]

What he adds is a more profound theistic motivation to persist in this form of self-expression. It is not just 'training' or a Kantian moral imperative which keeps us loyal through difficult times: it is the personal nature of the ultimate object of loyalty, God himself – as revealed in the promise-making God of the Old Testament and Jesus Christ of the New Testament. The motivating power of this God is unique. A God revealed as 'first person' means that the relation of loyalty to God is a personal relationship in which faithfulness can be grasped even in perplexing events. It is a personal relationship which enables a 'confidence in cosmic faithfulness'. It holds us to 'an assurance that there was one self-consistent intention in apparent evil as well as in apparent good'. It allows 'the postulate that God is faithful' to remain 'after every hypothesis about the mode of his faithfulness had broken down'.[23]

This theistic basis also radicalizes the motivation for *universal* loyalty. It does this by extending the scope of loyalty to everything the Creator God has made. It also demonstrates the significance of this universal loyalty for the self itself. The self which finds its ultimate loyalty in God-in-all-things will, *ipso facto*, be loyal in all its roles and relations in order to be a fulfilled self. So a proper theological framework means that the fulfilled self cannot, by definition, restrict its loyalties to a private sphere. A theology of loyalty requires public loyalties: it is an essentially public theology.

This is a fertile theological appropriation of loyalty. Yet interestingly it has not been much developed. Niebuhr himself did not fully explore its dimensions in relation to (for example) the doctrine of God. Others have tended to move swiftly to specific ethical implications, again without systematic theological discussion.[24] More theological work therefore needs to be done – not least because the social context of this new century still demands it. A society in which the self is increasingly fragmented and disconnected, both within itself and

from the wider narratives of life, is ripe for the rehabilitation
of fidelity: 'a message never more viable, more needed, and
more demanding than now'.[25] Equally, it will need to renew a
realistic, creative kind of fidelity – not blind loyalty. Royce,
Marcel and Niebuhr have set a scene for this. They offer useful
compass points on the map of definition and discourse. But a
fully theological account will need to reach further. It will
need to go both back behind them into the theological tradition and forwards to engage with the contemporary public
context of our own time. What follows is just one small contribution to this process: some talk about God to undergird a call
to faithfulness in a changing world.

2

DIVINE IDENTITY

Talk about God: some preliminaries

Talk about God is never easy. But it cannot endlessly be justifying itself to itself before it begins to address the world. God-talk cannot always wait to meet every prior theoretical objection before it ventures some public meaning. At some point it must begin and speak for itself. Some public meaning to divine identity has to be created in the very process of speaking, even when it cannot be assumed. In the same way, talk about God specifically as a basis for human living has to make sense without needing to prove all its credentials in advance. Thus only a brief theoretical preamble is offered in this chapter. Yes, there have to be some preliminaries because God-talk has become subject to so much suspicion; not least, it may be helpful simply to explain what we do *not* mean by 'talk of God' – which then clears the ground for positive possibilities of what God *does* mean. But it will be a quick move to this more substantive discussion, which is then developed in later chapters.

The sort of ground clearing which is most necessary relates to popular kinds of symbolic talk. A chief example is when 'God' is taken just as a symbolic way of talking about our ultimate meanings and purposes in life. The mathematical physicist who claims he may soon know the mind of God when he knows a unified theory of everything uses God symbolically in this way. By using the language of 'God' he implies he knows an ultimate meaning of everything. Any 'theory of everything' invites this outcome. This is *not* what we mean by public talk of God. Not only does it reduce the meaning of God: its ethical outcome is also problematic. A mathematical theory of elegance and balance too easily produces an aesthetic ethic which subordinates people to ideas, or art. A socio-biological evolutionary theory of random mutation and survival provides at best an ethic of mere pragmatism, at worst pure cynicism. Ancient philosophical theories of ultimate reality give similar hostages to moral and social fortune. A Heraclitean view that the ultimate nature of things is flux, dynamism, diversity, can be tracked through a whole range of unsatisfactory ethical programmes – from classical origins to Marxist ideas of inevitable dialectic and class conflict to the extreme individualism of postmodernism. The opposite Parmenidean view that the ultimate basis of this changing world is unity and static ideas produces a different kind of totalitarian ethic – from Plato's Republic to medieval Christendom to the ethics of modern scientific rationalism. Each of these theories of ultimate reality has been identified with God at various stages of its history.[1] None of them has proved ethically satisfactory.

The difficulty does not lie simply in some illicit philosophical jump from 'is' to 'ought' ('ultimate reality' to 'social ethics'). It lies in the notion of ultimate reality itself. Whenever it is invoked to justify a way of living which seems morally inadequate or counter-intuitive, it raises a doubt. Is it really an *ultimate* reality, explaining *everything*? We begin to suspect that calling it God is only a cloaking device, just meant to silence the doubt. So our moral unease deconstructs the divine symbol which was supposed to undergird the moral position in the first place. Straightforward theology often founders under the same scrutiny. Moral scruples about theology have always provided a more potent assault on belief than purely intellectual difficulties. This was a key issue in the nineteenth century and remains one of the most important lessons of the hermeneutic of suspicion, not just for theology but for all kinds of truth claims. We will never be able entirely to escape this suspicion that God is being invoked (or moulded) just to add authority to a world-view, and eliding the meaning of God merely with 'ultimate reality' makes it doubly hard.

So we must make it clear that the 'God' we refer to is not just the symbol of a particular scientific, social or philosophical programme. The meaning of God transcends this. It is the point which was signalled in the introduction. The God of Judaeo-Christian faith and historic theology does not belong to a singular social or intellectual context. This God incorporates the experience, praxis, reflection, social perspectives, of a myriad cross-cultural agendas. So while Christian theology is not and cannot be a view from nowhere, nor is it a view from just somewhere: it is a view from (and for) many times, places and perspectives. Its central doctrine of Christ-centredness and incarnation does not negate this but permits it. The very particularity of God's experience in Jesus of Nazareth is the basis for God to relate effectively to and from the experience of all other people's particularity.[2]

Talk of God is not, therefore, just some added value to a particular world-view. It *is* particular because it is about God revealed through the particularity of Christ, and it is provisional as all God-talk from a human viewpoint must be. But because its limitations are always tested through this immensely varied tradition of Christian praxis and theology its truth claims can be transcendent and universal. This should give more confidence that it has some *genuine* grasp on ultimate reality. Better still, it gives more purchase for this reality genuinely to grasp us.

Of course, this is still only a minimal exercise in ground-clearing. It still leaves much already assumed. To claim we can truly identify ultimate reality with the transcendent metaphysical reality of God remains a huge assumption. Talk based on a knowable and specific revelation of this God within space-time categories assumes even more. Such assumptions will still paralyse some theologians living under the shadow of Kant, who feel they cannot proceed to say anything substantive about God without more justification of how and why they can talk about God at all. So all sorts of other epistemological preliminaries could still be discussed before substantive theological statements are made.

But that is not for this book. I am willing to start on the assumption that Kant's boundary between the unknowable transcendent world and the knowable world of space–time is too starkly drawn.[3] I believe, in other words, that if God exists at all s/he must have made some sort of self-knowledge available to us, and so I can start talking about God on that basis without more ado. There is prima facie plausibility in this view. A transcendent but personal God is bound to have presented himself in some way within the categories of space, time, change, historicity – and I simply want to suggest some talk about God which is likely to make most sense in those terms. I am also willing to assume that moral and social consequences follow from this. For once we are really (not just symbolically) talking about ultimate reality, this is then not only legitimate but unavoidable. A truly ultimate reality must incorporate moral reality by definition, unless it is dogmatically reductive from the beginning. Is and ought must elide at this ultimate level, whatever separations there are in other discourse.

Divine identity

So much for the preliminaries – what now of the substantive talk itself? Who and what is this God revealed through the Judaeo-Christian tradition? If talk of ultimate reality is not enough, we shall want to say much more about the nature of this God for our talk about him to be any use. We need to know what belongs distinctively to the divine nature and being. In other words we need to know more of the divine *identity* – which might then shed light on our human identity and the way we should live.

To begin with we should simply say that who and what God is – divine identity – is the essential meaning of 'God' as distinct from anything or anyone else. As such it cannot radically change without ceasing to mean God, either by becoming many gods, or becoming something else, or becoming nothing. In any of these ways the meaning of God would collapse into self-contradiction. In that sense divine identity refers to a metaphysical claim about the *one* true God.[4] 'One' here does not necessarily refer to an inner simplicity and uniformity. That would preclude the Trinity. But it does define the enduring distinctiveness of this God (however complex) over against all other gods, all other reality, including finite and changing human reality. It therefore entails some sense of unity or constancy in divine identity which must remain the case through any process, time or change with which it is involved. This will be particularly important when we come to address meanings of God's own faithfulness. It also belongs to the meaning of God to be the source and ground of all other being, not simply another kind of being alongside others. This is a familiar point which means, among other things, that God cannot be thought of as 'a' person. It is another aspect of God's transcendence.

But alongside this it is still possible, and commonplace, to maintain that God is personal. God is consistently – though not exhaustively – experienced and conceived in this way. This was an important point for Niebuhr. It means, therefore, that we are always talking (at least analogously) of *personal* identity when we talk of divine identity. This comes close to the meaning of 'selfhood', as some strands of theology and philosophy use the term.[5] So the unique and enduring identity of God, while distinct, is not wholly unlike the meaning of human selfhood. To be sure, it remains only an analogy: we are not simply referring to God as a person, and this will be important in defining the differences as well as the similarities between divine and human personhood.[6] Nonetheless, the near interchangeability of terms is a helpful reminder of how closely the divine-human analogy can operate. This God is not just metaphysically one and constant, but *personally* one and constant.

In this way we are always bound within a paradox when we are pressing for the meaning of God. On the one hand we want the meaning of the one transcendent and constant God, not simply a reductive projection of our own finite categories of experience. This requires some talk of God's transcendence of finitude, time, change: divine identity, qua divine, demands this. On the other hand, we can only look for this meaning in some sort of personal reality which we have encountered as personal beings ourselves. This requires talk of a personal relationship of God to these categories of time and change in which our own personal identity is found and formed: *personal* divine identity demands that too.

Divine action as access to divine identity

Such a paradoxical relation of divine to human reality is important. Although problematic, it points to the place where we will find a point of access. We must have some access to this sort of transcendent reality – and it is the paradox of its relation to our own selfhood which permits this. How is this?

The answer lies in the notion of personal action. This is certainly how we know the identity of others in human inter-relations. They may be truly other and transcend us in important ways, but we can still know them – through their actions. 'Intentional action is an important way, possibly the only real way a person has of extending his identity and relating himself to the . . . world.'[7] A moment's thought confirms this. If I can frame no kind of purposive action in any way nor engage in reciprocal purposive relations with anyone else, then my identity remains private, inaccessible and ultimately solipsistic. Whatever meaning remains in my identity is self-enclosed. Intentional action therefore becomes the 'public' meaning of personal identity. Our transcendent selves become accessible in our action. A fortiori this will also be true of divine identity. Any personal identity of God accessible in this temporal world is bound to involve some notion of intentional divine action, especially if 'action' is understood as incorporating more general notions of divine self-expression. Elsewhere I have argued this in more detail. There are conceptual difficulties for maintaining the notion of agency for a truly transcendent reality, but they are not decisive and need not deter us. This is partly because the meaning of agency can be qualified (e.g. as non-bodily) without losing all meaning. It is also because it does not have to displace other theological notions of God's self-expression – such as his embodiment in the world, panentheistic models of divine being and presence, process models of divine 'lure' – all of which mitigate some of the conceptual problems. In one way or another, therefore, intentional action can remain pivotal for *any* personal identity, including divine identity. God's identity is known and expressed in his action.[8]

Distinctive divine action: love and faithfulness

The main 'master' actions of God grasped within the Judaeo-Christian tradition are evident. They have to do with creation and redemption. God is known as Creator and Redeemer of the world generally, and of peoples and individuals more specifically. Incarnation is the specific form through which this overall action takes place. If we want to know what sort of actions these are, this need not involve discussion about their causal mechanics: there is ample discussion elsewhere about *how* God might be conceived acting in this world in relation to its natural causes and its social and moral structures.[9] It is more a question of *what* than how: i.e. what is the overall intentionality of these actions through time and change, the moral substance of them, and the distinctive personal identity this conveys. So it is a question of divine *character*, but also more than this: if identity has to do with the meaning of God's distinctive nature and being it is a question about the essential constituents of divine selfhood, not just dispositions of character.

In this context 'love' is then the most immediate and obvious answer. Love is always an overall intention. It is consistently declared to be at the heart of God's selfhood and action. God moves in love towards others in his actions in the world, and this is an expression of the essential movement of love within the trinitarian structure of his own being. God *is* love, and that is how he fulfils himself in time and eternity. It is at the heart of divine identity, expressed pre-eminently in the

Christ event. This logic and meaning of love in divine being, personhood and action, is a well trawled field of theological exploration.[10]

However, it is also important to specify the meaning of this love – and especially in all our talk of God relating to the world. What *sort* of love defines the identity of God? Talk of love, like talk of God, even at the formal level, begs this question. It is part of the quest for meaning. And it is here that the central conviction of this book, in its theology as well as its ethics, finds its main point of departure. A key defining feature of divine love-in-action is faithfulness. Faithfulness is so often what this love means.

With notable exceptions in Barth and Pannenberg faithfulness has not featured greatly in the doctrine of God in systematic theology. Niebuhr, as we saw, did not develop it in that way. Yet it has good reason to be considered. The main narratives of divine action in the biblical traditions signal its importance. As we shall see, the purposeful action of God *is* faithfulness and promise keeping. Crucially, it appears in these narratives to be the form that love takes specifically in relation to time and change. In doctrine the essential meaning of divine identity as personal unity and constancy points clearly towards faithfulness. It implies that faithfulness, like love, defines the meaning of God in the very structure of divine being, not just in dispositions of character. Faithfulness also proves particularly fruitful in key areas (such as theodicy) where more general notions of love falter.

All this suggests that divine faithfulness is ripe for more consideration. It is where talk of God touches his identity, and ours, at its heart. So it is to this we now turn.

3

DIVINE FAITHFULNESS

Divine faithfulness in biblical traditions

The centrality of divine faithfulness in biblical narrative is clear. In the Old Testament the notion of covenant is determinative for conveying this faithfulness. The cause of the old covenant is *'ahabah'*: God's electing love. The means of carrying this out is characteristically expressed by *'chesed'*: i.e. covenant love which is frequently translated as faithfulness. 'The word means faithfulness rather than kindness, for . . . it involves, in almost every case, a substratum of fixed, determined, almost stubborn steadfastness.'[1] This can be found most clearly expressed in Hosea, Jeremiah, Amos. It is frequently paired with *'met'* (truth): i.e. the truthfulness and trustworthiness of keeping a promise. In the Old Testament narrative this is repeatedly sought for and has to be rediscovered, especially in times of national or personal difficulty and disaster. This is particularly apparent in the psalms. It also has to be reaffirmed in the face of human rebellion and disloyalty. Faced with the recurring dilemma of Israel's failure to meet God's demand for righteousness and the possibility that God would not continue to save his people, the prophets were driven to find further dimensions of God's *chesed*. God must be marrying mercy to justice in different ways. Remnant theology was an important consequence of this: a new way of squaring the circle in favour of God's fundamental faithfulness. Hence: 'this dynamic, whereby one must discover God's loyal love all over again at each new crisis, seems central to God's ways with humankind as the biblical authors present it'.[2]

Much the same dynamic emerges through another dominant Old Testament motif: the pattern of promise and fulfilment which is integral to major types of covenant.[3] Thus Von Rad: 'From Abraham to Malachi, Israel was kept constantly in motion because of what God said and did. . . . she was always in one way or other in an area of tension constituted by promise and fulfilment.'[4] When fulfilment is clearly experienced it is recorded as a sign of God's faithfulness. When fulfilment is only experienced as partial or pending, Israel has to move through each new historical event by a process of reinterpretation or expectation of some further revelation. So while Israel's perception of divine faithfulness and promise-keeping is by no means unequivocal, it is always reincorporated in new events, and divine faithfulness continually re-experienced.[5]

All this suggests an inextricable relation between the early biblical notions of faithfulness with temporality, flux, process, change. God has to be sought for and has to demonstrate himself by faithful acts, repeatedly, *through time*. Pannenberg makes the same point generally about the meaning of divine identity in all religion:

> neither in monotheistic nor in polytheistic religions does the endorsement of religious ideas of deity take place in the form of a single, definite act, though there might well be specific events and experiences which either shake or permanently establish belief . . . Gods that become objects of worship are not just entities of the moment . . . Since the process of experience both in individual life and in the history of peoples is open to an unknown future, and the reality of the world may of itself encounter us in different and surprising forms. . . . the question of the power of the deity is constantly posed afresh. God is believed to be the same over the years . . . The power ascribed to him *must prove itself again and again*.[6]

Ernest Nicholson picks up this dynamic specifically in relation to Old Testament notions of covenant. Against those who see it primarily as a social institution, Nicholson emphasizes its character as a theological idea, a vision of God as he relates to his people. There can be no presumption of this relationship as if it is a fixed order of being, a given reality based on some ontological equivalence between divine and human. Instead, it is a dynamic relationship of choice, to be freely expressed by God as well as his people. As such it requires a process of renewal through time. Thus:

> so far from being a social institution the covenant represents the refusal of prophets . . . to encapsulate Yahweh's rela-tionship with his people in institutions. . . . it depends on a moral commitment on both sides *which needs to be continu-ally reaffirmed in faithful conduct.*[7]

This covenant relationship is not exclusive to the people of Israel. Its chief role is to describe God's particular bond with them, but extensions are suggested. The covenant with Noah is extended to 'every living creature'(Genesis 9.17). The foun-dational patriarchal covenant with Abraham is closely associ-ated with Abraham's vocation to be a blessing to many nations (cf. Genesis 12,15,17). Exegesis of such narratives may be arguable, but in the overall hermeneutic of biblical theologies they remain important signposts for an incipient universal-ism.

In the New Testament covenant does not dominate to quite the same extent. Warnings against reading it into the New Testament in an inflated way are not uncommon in the battle-ground of biblical studies. But it is by no means absent. The covenant pattern of promise and fulfilment is explicitly endorsed in the Epistle to the Hebrews and rooted in the constancy of the character of God himself 'in order to make the unchanging nature of his promise very clear to the heirs of what was promised'.[8] A new covenant is explicitly established in Christ and, in some sense, *as* Christ.[9] As such, it shares at least something of the temporal dynamic of the old covenant and connects crucially with this dynamic of promise and fulfil-ment. Christ is pre-eminently both promise and fulfilment. He expresses divine faithfulness both for the present and the future, and therefore re-establishes the divine commitment through time.

This new act in Christ is represented as different in kind from all previous acts. It is inclusive of them and uniquely a fulfilment of them, both retrospectively and prospectively. In Pannenberg's terms it is one of those specific events in a religion which establishes a belief and a new reality to make sense of all other beliefs. It has a constitutive role, not just a revelatory role.[10] Nonetheless it is still a new act which must be and is continually re-expressed in other acts *through time*. Hence the New Testament correlation of the new covenant with the Spirit who continues to work in the world, and with the Kingdom which is realized in the acts and events of this world, as well as the next.[11] The faithfulness of Jesus himself is another feature of the New Testament narrative and theology which shares a similar pattern. Whatever exegetical difficulties are involved in interpreting the faith *of* Christ in Pauline theology, the general structure of his (saving) faithfulness in Hebrews theology is clear enough: he is a faithful high priest through what he suffered, in the process of time.

Deeper dimensions of faithfulness, developing Old Testament *chesed*, are expressed through its New Testament counterpart of 'grace'. Grace expresses the same sense of an initiative and free choice of God which is not bound in institutions but rooted in the sort of dynamic relationship with people which Christ expressed – and which calls forth the continually renewable response of faith. Its other counterpart is 'love' (*agape*). This love is, again, timeful: it is faithfulness and persistence, even and especially in the face of sin. This is at the heart of the New Testament passion and resurrection narrative, the climax of the covenant. Grace and love both function like this in the theological analysis of Romans where Paul struggles to determine how God could express his own righteousness in the act of mercy: the act of justification by divine grace, through faith. This is also the substance of Paul's covenant theology in Romans 9—11 where Israel's rejection and unfaithfulness do not subvert the deeper faithfulness of

God: there is the promise of yet another new act to graft Gentile and Jew back in together. In other words, this grace of God has a unilateral meaning. It does not depend on reciprocity, even though it always seeks it.

In this way grace and love radicalize the meaning of covenant. They give both moral and ontological priority to the free gift of divine initiative and persistence. The mutuality and reciprocity of human response is not denied, but it is reordered in a subordinate role. The overwhelming emphasis is on a divine faithfulness which continues to have meaning and creative potential apart from reciprocity.

These Pauline texts have been profoundly important in shaping the doctrine and history of the Church. They were pivotal in Luther's appropriation of Augustine's doctrine of grace, with its radical theological and political implications for the Church of his time. They were central to the Reformation, and have continued to shape theological and ecclesiological debate to an extraordinary degree. The Lutheran extrapolation of a core doctrine of justification has been described as 'the real theological centre of the theological system of the Christian church', an abiding touchstone of theological truth, a canon within the canon.[12]

This doctrinal history has involved serious misreadings on the way. The doctrine has been construed as an attack on supposed Jewish legalism, exploited to justify antisemitism, oblivious to notions of grace already amply contained within Judaism. It has led to an abstract, forensic notion of divine justice, which required satisfying in equally impersonal terms. But the significance and staying power of the doctrine does not depend on its distortions. The heart of it is a different concern altogether: to establish a central feature of divine identity as *righteousness* (a cognate of 'justify' in Greek). God's righteousness must somehow be explicated in relation to both Jew and Gentile, obedience and disobedience. Judgement and wrath, as well as grace and mercy, are all integral stages in the fulfilment of this righteousness. That is the dominating theme of these Pauline texts, especially the Epistle to the Romans. And righteousness is, precisely, a relational and covenantal

term virtually synonymous with faithfulness. The righteousness of God lies in his unswerving commitment to remain true
to himself in his mutual covenant relations and obligations
with his people.[13] This is also implied in its close link with
divine power to succeed. The righteousness of God is 'the
power of God for salvation'. In other words it is the faithfulness at the heart of divine righteousness which underwrites
the outcome of the whole salvation history with which God is
engaged.

As with the Old Testament, none of this should be read
exclusively. God's people of both the old and new covenants
are the main subject of the narrative of divine action, but that
story is not self-contained. At key points it functions as a sign
for the whole world. Thus Paul's theology of history in
Romans 9–11 climaxes in an entirely open-ended paeon of
praise: the God who is covenanted to the final salvation of
Israel not only grafts Jews and Gentiles together but reveals
himself ultimately as 'source, guide and goal of *all* that is'
(Romans 11.36).

Divine faithfulness and the doctrine of God

Such biblical notions and stories of divine faithfulness are of
central importance. They must be taken into account in any
adequate Christian doctrine of God. But how has this been
done, and how adequately?

A number of major contemporary theological concerns at
least imply notions of divine faithfulness. Recent preoccupation with the doctrine of the Trinity provides an obvious basis.
The revival of the ancient doctrine of *perichoresis* produces a
fertile conceptual structure. God is God only as a mutual and
eternal interpenetration of Father, Son and Holy Spirit. They
constitute each other's being, and the divine being as such, by
their relations. In other words, divine identity is essentially
constituted as a constant ('faithful') interrelationship. This
offers, at least potentially, a model of both flux and stability,
relationality and commitment, all cohering in God and providing a similar pattern for God's relationship with the world.

When this is contrasted with monadic, hierarchical and monarchical models, it readily feeds contemporary theological concerns, not least feminism. Trinitarian relationalism, particularly when it is incorporated in the world's relations in a panentheistic way, 'resonates profoundly with feminist theology . . . a critical mass of those Christian feminists who are willing to construct metaphors of the divine do so out of their analysis of subjectivity as co-constituted by its relations'.[14] Such relationism does not stand unchallenged, even within feminism, but it remains pervasive – and it is a ready correlate of notions of faithfulness which require this combination of constancy, commitment, and dynamism. Much the same implication can be drawn from liberation and green theologies which emphasize essential divine commitment to historical and natural processes. Such commitment implies a corresponding structure of dynamic commitment in the being of God himself. In a similar way eschatological theologies which insist on the necessary, radical consummation of all things imply the essential faithfulness which God is expressing to creation.[15]

But what of explicit and sustained treatment of divine faithfulness in systematic theology? Historically, notions of faithfulness featured significantly in a good deal of Puritan theology, and Reformed theology in general.[16] They were a major presupposition of the doctrine of providence which dominated the theology of the time. But this tradition has not persisted in much mainstream systematic theology. Nor did its largely non-metaphysical methodology encourage much reflection on fundamental ontological questions about God which are raised by the notion of faithfulness – such as God's relation to temporality.

The reason why faithfulness has not played its full part in systematic doctrine is not hard to fathom. It has to do, precisely, with the intrinsic temporality of the notion and the difficulties this would raise within many major metaphysical frameworks of historical theology. Most obviously, the classic foundations for theology in Thomism and the older neo-platonic traditions are so wary of change in God that their treatment of God's relation to temporality and change tends to be strained through impersonal metaphors of timeless relations. This does not fit easily with the language of faithfulness and its dynamic of personal action, achieving goals and realizing intentions through time and change. Thus when Aquinas writes on the existence and nature of God in the *Summa*, there is often an uneasy mix of metaphors. There is a striking image of the extension of God throughout space and time as a 'mobile wisdom'. This is

> a way of saying that wisdom spreads its own likeness throughout the length and breadth of things . . . we talk of God's wisdom sallying forth as it were and moving into things. It is as though we talked of the sun sallying forth on earth when its light rays touched earth. [And this is the explanation Dionysius gives, when he says that every emanation of the divine majesty comes to us set in motion by the Father of lights.][17]

It is an image which could easily be read as a metaphor of faithfulness: i.e. a divine presence in and commitment to all that is. But it is notable that the images of movement (the 'sallying forth') are less dominant than the static or impersonal images ('wisdom', 'light', 'sun'). The metaphysical constraints lying behind this are familiar. They involve notions of divine perfection which exclude any movement, change, or goal-seeking. These would imply unrealized potentiality in the divine being (which is pure act). As we are reminded in the same section: 'all change has a goal, so that things which have already achieved their ultimate goal will not change'.[18]

This is by no means all that can be said about Aquinas, nor by him. Elsewhere he tells us: 'God is in all things . . . as an agent is present to that upon which it works.' And 'God causes this effect in things [i.e the effect of being creatures] not only when they first begin to be, but as long as they are preserved in being.'[19] Here there is clearly some sort of metaphor of faithfulness, with agency and persistence explicitly stated. It is a relation of pure act and immutable being to temporal reality which a sympathetic critic can expound as 'supremely dynamic (pure act to created act), utterly intimate (a relation between God as he is in himself and the creature as it is in itself), and unbreakably enduring (it can never be severed)'.[20] It raises the notorious logical difficulty of how a *real* reciprocal relation of an unchanging to a changing reality can be construed, but even this can be defended, however arguably.[21]

Yet the strain of the metaphors remains. The underlying metaphysic still exerts its pressure. The metaphors of agency and persistence may be employed, but they are only used in a relation which is effecting a general ontological category, such as 'createdness'. So they have to be heavily translated to do justice to the language of faithfulness which is effecting not just the category of createdness but a profound and dynamic personal relation. It is not that Thomist theology has no inclination to express faithfulness. But it can only do so in a difficult and grudging way which does not sit comfortably with other essential categories of the divine identity. Its proper concern never to short-change divine transcendence will always create tension with the temporality of biblical narrative.

This does not mean that the classical strand of theological tradition is a dead end. It simply highlights the need to pay attention to other parts of the tradition as well. Theological tradition should always permit other perspectives without needing to discard everything about previous attempts: this is the nature of a tradition trying to deal with ultimate reality and mystery. So this naturally leads us to other giants of systematic theology. There is Karl Barth, for example – closer to older Puritan theologies in many respects but also more critically engaged than they were with the Thomist tradition and its ontological concerns.

Barth deals with divine faithfulness in section II:1.6 of the *Church Dogmatics*, directly associating it with divine identity. It is subsumed under one of the perfections of divine freedom, as 'constancy'.[22] The divine freedom is the freedom of God always and in every circumstance to be himself and confirm himself as himself. It is the freedom of God to remain the one he is, secure in his personal identity. Constancy, therefore, is the correlate of this freedom. He will be himself again and again. But what is this divine identity that is constantly fulfilled? It is a divine life which includes *in itself* 'the fullness of difference, movement, will, decision, action . . . which He lives in eternal self-repetition and self-affirmation.'[23] Here Barth distinguishes his position from that of Augustine, who retains a notion of rest within God in himself, however active in his relations to the world. Here we also find the critical basis for a real divine relation to the world of change and temporality. Because God is not just the origin of all movement, time and change, but is in himself the fullness of difference, change and movement, then a real and reciprocal relation with such a world is ontologically and logically less problematic. Theologically, this space is defined by the Trinity.

The question still arises whether it is theologically problematic for movement and difference to be conceived within a perfect God. But this is mitigated if it is the *fullness* of movement, change, and difference within God. This gives meaning to 'new' divine acts in the world's history including God's changing action and reaction in relation to human sin: 'constancy involves a real history . . . a history in relation to [fallen] creation, which means new and different ways of acting'.[24] Equally, these do not add something new to the divine identity in being or nature, for this already includes the fullness of all change and movement. The new acts in the human world may well be decisive for our grasp of the divine identity, but they are always, ontologically speaking, a repetition or expression of the fullness of the divine identity rather than an addition to it. Thus it remains true that 'God is what He is in eternal actuality. He never is it only potentially'.[25] This means there is a kind of immutability in the divine being, although it is the immutability of always and fully being this divine self of movement and change. That is why Barth prefers the word constancy to immutability:

> God's constancy – which is a better word than the suspiciously negative immutability – is the constancy of his knowing, willing and acting and therefore of his person. It

is the continuity, undivertability and indefatigableness in which God both is himself and also performs His work. . . . continually making it His work.[26]

Barth links this sort of dynamic constancy with the true meaning of divine omnipotence. Power should not be considered in its own terms then applied to God. True power is defined by who and what God is, not vice versa. In van den Brink's terms, philosophical concepts of omnipotence which were originally abstracted from a religious context must not then be reapplied to God *ad extra*: they only take their true meaning from the divine character, and cannot add meaning to it.[27] Divine power is therefore defined by this key category of divine constancy, which in turn has so closely defined the divine identity. As such it must be considered not just as a physical possibility or causal power but as a moral requirement of faithfulness. It must be seen as a correlate of constancy, the power to always and entirely be himself in every respect and every circumstance. This means that whatever God wills to do to be himself he can do, and what he actually does he is willing to do. Otherwise he would not be fully himself. In short, if God *is* faithful he *can* and *will* be faithful. This is one of those thick theological statements which sound suspiciously like tauto-logy but which actually add meaning in the saying. It is the dogmatic expression of the Pauline link between righteousness-faithfulness and 'the power of God for salvation'.

This kind of ontology features in even more radical form in Pannenberg – another twentieth-century systematic theologian who pays some attention to divine faithfulness and connects it explicitly with divine identity. Pannenberg treats it as an attribute of the love of God. Like righteousness, with which he connects it, it defines the very identity of God. It is 'the identity and consistency of the eternal God in his turning in love to his creatures'. It expresses 'his constancy in the actual process of time and history . . . in his covenant . . . his promises . . . the orders of creation'.[28] This is not just construed as some sort of economic identity of God in his relations to then world, unrelated to his essential being. As with Barth it means a becoming, historicity and contingency in God, which is 'the expression of his eternity in the process of time'.[29] This is constitutive of his eternal identity, rather than some kind of contingent extra to it, for 'only through faithfulness does something lasting arise'.[30] In Pannenberg's terms this constitutive element is understood as the eschatological consummation of a process where there is *coincidence* of time and eternity, rather than a straightforward take-over. This ontology is explicitly contrasted with classical doctrines of immutability in which the changeless and timeless God cannot receive change into his own being.

None of this goes unchallenged, of course. Both Barth and, to a lesser extent, Pannenberg have been taken to task in the very core of this ontology. Their concern to expound faithfulness in this way has been taken as a sort of metaphysical failure of nerve. By their construals of constancy, repetition, and consistency they are said to have offered a notion of ethical immutability, but not ontological immutability. But can ethical immutability be sustained if it is not founded on some truly unchanging ontology? And must not some sort of ontological changelessness be construed for God to be truly transcendent *as God*, rather than merely a projection of this passing world? This is Thomas Weinandy's criticism. He presses it home like this:

> The obvious motivation behind these theologians is to maintain both God's goodness and love, and his vital interaction with and in the world. Ethical immutability seems to allow both and there is no doubt that Yahweh is revealed within the Hebrew Scriptures as ethically immutable. However, by making God merely ethically immutable, it is difficult to see what is the metaphysical foundation for his immutable goodness and love.[31]

His own solution is to re-enter the metaphysics of the Thomist world to show how it can, after all, logically sustain real interaction between the immutable God and the world. In this way: when God acts in the world this does not mean that God has undergone some change, but that change occurs in the thing or person so they are newly related to God as he is.

Weinandy's proposal may not convince.[32] It is also moot whether it is even necessary as a manoeuvre: Barth's ontology of perfect becoming in being *is* a kind of ontological constancy. But the Thomist challenge at least has this merit: it continues a conversation about divine faithfulness in which the transcendence and ultimacy of metaphysical foundations are kept high on the agenda. It maintains a doctrine of God's being which includes the strongest possible sense of divine transcendence over against temporality, change and suffering, whatever else may also be said about his immanence. I have every sympathy with this[33]. There must be some sort of ontological foothold beyond the world for his effective action in the world and as the basis for redeeming the world, ultimately, from suffering. This is a moral as well as a metaphysical imperative, connected with theodicy. It is a demand of responsible creative love that it has the metaphysical capacity to fulfil its own being-for-others, its aspirations for the beloved. It is another sense in which God must be able to be himself in order to be truly God.

Such concerns surface with particular poignancy in Frances Young's extraordinary book, *Face to Face*. In its collision between narrative, personalist theology (including the narrative of her personal suffering) and her patristic background, the former did not entirely win out. Precisely to make sense of temporality and suffering she is driven to explore ways of being *beyond* it.[34] This seems to indicate that some sort of negation, or radical transcendence, of temporality and change within God does have to be maintained alongside their affirmation. In that sense the continued pressure of the Thomist tradition, in conversation with a more Barthian theology, is constructive. It reminds us that any theology which struggles to speak of transcendent God in relation to temporal reality will always need some critique from its conversation partners. This is true even of Process Theology, which builds its whole edifice of a bi-polar God precisely on the pivot of this issue, trying to contain a whole answer within its own metaphysic. Even this, in my view, fails on its own.[35]

Apophatic traditions also provide help in the conversation. Early mystical traditions, such as that of Pseudo-Dionysius, offer useful insights into this difficult business of holding negation and affirmation together in our talk of God. They remind us that theological language about transcendence, if it is truly reaching beyond itself, includes the radical double-negative: in the face of the ultimate mystery of God, negation must even negate itself if it is not to foreclose on the mystery.[36] This does not wholly sideline reason. It is a 'reasonable' reflection on mystery and transcendence which itself suggests the need for these paradoxes. For if we are speaking truly of a transcendent God, rather than just projecting our own experience, reason itself demands that we always have to say these two things. First, that God is not simply ourselves, or this world, writ large: s/he is not bound by time, change, particularity, personhood in the same way that we are. But second, we cannot say either that God is simply without time, change, particularity, personhood. That would be equally limiting. This gives back some sense of time and change even *within* ultimate timelessness and changelessness. We have to say that he is not timeless or changeless as much as we have to say she is not time-bound or changing – and in that sense it allows for affirmation within the negation. In this way the coincidence of apparently polar opposites is held within language and reason, as well as the mystical experiences which lie behind it. It gives real opportunities for speaking both of a God who acts in time and a divine transcendence of all time and change.[37]

In such ways, therefore, the notion of faithfulness proves a catalyst for exploring key mysteries in the doctrine of God. Not only does it dominate the identity of the God revealed in Judaeo-Christian biblical narrative – it also proves itself in doctrinal reflection to be central to both divine nature and being. It does not feature as much as it should in systematic theology – but when it is given due weight it illuminates important questions of ontology, the being of God in relation to the world and himself. It presses theology to redefine immutability and eternity, but also to rehabilitate them. It insists on holding together categories of radical transcendence and radical historicity. It refuses to short-change the paradox on either side. In this sense it is constructive in the business of formulating credible doctrines of God, not reductive. It informs the mystery and expands it. It is central, therefore, to divine identity.

Divine faithfulness and theodicy

This book is not setting out to offer a systematic theology, so the relation of faithfulness to other specific areas of doctrine will not be dealt with here. The aim to establish theological foundations for human faithfulness should be served well enough by just this outline of biblical traditions and the doctrine of God. However, there is one more issue underlying systematic theology which presses for more attention. It is a ghost which haunts all theological talk and always needs to be faced in public theology: the question of theodicy. Does the notion of divine faithfulness have any particular role to play here?

I believe it does. It is in relation to theodicy that faithfulness offers a good deal of fresh meaning. It may even prove itself more fruitful than the generic notion of love – and to treat it just as an attribute of love, as Pannenberg does, may be inadequate. In theodicy faithfulness demonstrates itself with special clarity not just as one attribute of divine love amongst others, but as the defining feature of love within temporal reality.

This arises directly out of what has gone before. It derives from both the biblical narratives of covenant and their ontological implications in the doctrine of God. The former suggested that the essence of biblical covenant faithfulness was the unfolding of God's commitment to his people through time. As such it had to be continually renewed. Its meaning and possibility were established by particular events, but it also required a repetition of this meaning through the historical process, reaffirmed in the face of new occasions of rebellion, sin, suffering and evil. But the latter also reminded us that if God is to be truly God in this way, other conditions must be met. Namely, whatever change, movement, suffering are involved in us and God, this process must also be part of an eternal completion, a perfection, a completed story. In Aquinas's terms, it is pure act with no potential. In Barth's terms, it is always perfectly fulfilled potential, a perfect becoming in being. In Pannenberg's terms, it is a process and history of God in time which is always subject to the eschatological consummation. But in any of these different terms the one overall implication is the same. *It means that the notion of God's faithfulness drives us in two directions at once. It has a sort of intrinsic bi-polarity. It takes us uncompromisingly into the reality of actual historical process to seek signs of his continued commitment to us. But at the same time it does this always and only in the light of a whole story, whose beginning and end radically transcend us at any one moment.* All this is the clear implication of finding the basis for divine identity in an eternal unity, of which faithfulness through time is the essential historical expression.

It is notable that theodicy has struggled most when it has focused only on one or other of these directions. On the one hand, concentration on the overall unity of things, the higher harmony which Ivan Karamazov renounced, will always founder on the grit of actual events. The experience of great evil and suffering is not neutralized by construing it as the broken eggs needed to make some future utopian omelette. It is not enough. God is not justified like that. On the other hand, radical historicism which immerses itself exclusively in the actuality and particularity of terrible events also fails. It becomes literally rooted to the spot so that belief in God reduces to belief in a god whose own historical suffering and vulnerability is itself ultimate. 'God' becomes just our present experience rather than the totality of experience. This is where we more usually find ourselves in our current climate of post-modernism, which considers any larger story problematic. We are preoccupied with our immediate selves unconnected with any wider perspective. Pannenberg picks up Rahner's striking image of 'the blank face' of God to make just this point:

If the word is like a blank face to us it reminds us by its very strangeness of the lack of meaning in modern life, *in which the theme of life's unity and totality is missing* and the wholeness of human existence has become an unanswered question.[38]

Crucially, the notion of faithfulness will not let us settle here. It always drives theodicy in both directions. It points to meaning in the whole, completed pattern of life, as well as the particulars of life. By definition it is itself only in its commitment to the *whole* story, as well as in every particularity of the story. In other words, if God is to be justified at all, he is justified only by inhabiting both eternity and time. He is truly himself only as he fully immerses himself in heaven and earth. The fullest meaning only emerges from both, the ultimate and penultimate.

The notion of love could do something similar, when properly understood. The meaning of love will embrace all that faithfulness conveys, and more, when fully read off from the whole biblical narrative and theological tradition. But the specific notion of faithfulness is often a vital safeguard to that full meaning when it is threatened by the reductionism of current culture. This tends to suck love into an exclusively existential and occasional meaning. The love of current discourse is authenticated in early closure, rather than promise, trust, futurity and transcendence. It quickly becomes a notion of moments much more than a notion to do with the totality of a long story. The effect on building a theology of the love of God is inevitable. All that can be known of love when past and future events are closed off too soon is its vulnerability and powerlessness. To put it another way, it is built out of the cross alone, closed off from the resurrection. The huge influence on English theology (and theodicy) of a book like W. H. Vanstone's *Love's Endeavour Love's Expense* is a case in point. It is a theology built on a phenomenology of love in just this way – and it fails as a result to be fully theological.[39] The point can be extended from theodicy to more general ethical theory. The susceptibility of love, both divine and human, to a hermeneutics of short-term ethical occasionism is illustrated by another influential book. Joseph Fletcher's *Situation Ethics* can offer 'the most loving thing' as a guide to moral behaviour only by atomizing each situation being assessed.[40] Traditions, principles and rules which derive from connected and accumulated meaning over a period of time are relegated to low status, compared to the sovereignty of the present situation.[41]

Faithfulness, with its powerful push to repetition, constancy and overall unity, fares much better at just these points where love is inclined to falter. In terms of theodicy, it holds the meanings of God open, refusing to foreclose, requiring total responsibility for all his creation, however hard that is to conceive at any one moment. In terms of ethics, as we shall see, it will require an answering sense of *long-term* responsibility from us.

The shape of divine faithfulness: setting an agenda

In these ways, therefore, the faithfulness of God's identity in himself shapes his relations with the world. God expresses faithfulness both through time and change, and in the completion of time and change. This treats both the penultimate and ultimate meanings of our existence with seriousness. It is a commitment of love undeterred by times of unresponsiveness or disobedience, but not unaffected by them. There is dynamism and responsiveness in this divine faithfulness, as well as stability and constancy.

Specifically, and especially when faced with sin and evil, faithfulness takes the shape of the divine act(s) of grace, mercy and wrath, which constitute 'justification' within the overall process of salvation. Like love itself, this originates in the freedom, initiative and trinitarian life of God, but is other-orientated, seeking the good of the world, not simply self-fulfilling. It expresses the divine identity, therefore, as a purposive, dynamic, goal-seeking activity. All this is uniquely expressed in particular events and actions (the Exodus, the Christ event), and it is uniquely grasped by particular peoples (Israel, the Christian Church). Equally, what is experienced in these particulars extends to every other particular too: to other peoples, and to the whole creation. Finally, being *divine* faithfulness, it is intrinsically related to divine power eventually to *achieve* these purposes. This is a moral requirement for a sense of divine omnipotence, which only makes sense of divine agency in both the totality and the completion of time and change. Divine identity is essentially constituted in these ways. All this emerges as the shape of God's (faithful) being in and for the world.

This clearly sets the theological context for the shape of human response and human living. In Niebuhr's terms, it shows the ultimate shape and meaning of life (God) to which we must respond in our life of time and change. Responding to this sort of God will matter supremely as we try to live truthfully as the sort of people we are. If human identity is related in any way at all to divine identity then we are bound to take such faithfulness into account for our own fulfilment. It means that faithfulness will matter for our identity just as it does for the divine identity, as Royce and Marcel have insisted. Moreover, specific social and ethical implications for human action and response will naturally flow from this, as we shall see.

But first there must be some attempt to clarify this connection between divine and human identity. What is the relationship between the two? How does the analogy work? What *is* human identity anyway? Talk about ourselves is not necessarily to be taken for granted, any more than talk about God. In other words, some sort of theological anthropology is needed before moving on to more specific ethical issues. That is what now follows.

4

HUMAN IDENTITY

Talk about ourselves: some preliminaries

Talk about ourselves might be expected to be easier than talk about God. But human identity is no simple subject. Its complexities are reflected in the varied way the term is used. 'Personal identity' has different meanings in different discourse. It is also confused by interchangeable use of two other terms closely related with it: selfhood and personhood.

It is not going to be possible to tidy up this terminological playing field entirely. Meanings of words are too determined by wider cultural contexts of use and resonance. No single discourse can hope to prescribe effectively for others. All I can do is indicate how I shall use the terms.

Defining human identity

I will take human identity in a parallel way to divine identity: i.e. as an inclusive term covering all significant and distinctive aspects of human being. As such it includes biologically determined aspects of our nature and being to do with sex, race, kinship and bodily identity. It includes culturally determined aspects of human being, such as gender identity, nationality, social role. It also involves character and disposition. With socially constructed aspects of identity, some elements will involve personal choice, others will be wholly determined. 'Identity' incorporates all of these aspects of our being, but does not reduce to any one of them.

Personhood will mean the most fundamental constituent of

identity: a necessary (but not necessarily sufficient) condition for any human identity. I will take it as a continuous 'substratum' or 'thread' of being which persists throughout all human lives and distinguishes them from other creatures. It does not have to be identified with the dualistic notion of a soul, rationality, moral awareness, nor any particular physiological phenomenon such as brain activity – though it may relate to all these. I am not pursuing that debate here. It *will* mean something intrinsically relational: our personhood exists by its relation to other persons, divine and human. However, that does not mean it is reducible to mere 'relation'; there must be some unique centre with which to relate to others which is not just the 'relation' itself (the importance of this will become apparent later when the significance of reciprocity is considered).[1]

Self or *selfhood* I shall use simply as the individuated and reflexive term of identity. It is that sense of identity (inluding personhood) which belongs uniquely to you or me and is experienced by you and me. The fact that it is unique is highly significant. It denotes both the singular nature of our self-awareness and the objective irreplaceability of each human individual.

Defined like this, human identity refers to both actual and potential human being. It describes something which is the case for us, and which might be the case. It incorporates unchanging and changing aspects of our being, some which are given and some which are socially constructed or personally chosen. That which changes can affect our identity and our sense of self profoundly: it can bring development or decay, desirable goals or disaster. But the enduring fact of personhood remains throughout. These notions are not uncontested, as we shall see. Even Christian views of personhood are wary of some definitions of this enduring centre. For Al McFadyen there is no 'substantial personal core' or 'pre-social substance' within us which endures.[2] Instead, the centre is established only by a socially acquired belief. This emerges through a process of 'sedimentation' through our interrelations with others. In my view this can become too weak as a definition of personhood, potentially reducible to the abstraction of being *merely* a relation.[3] But the fact that McFadyen himself would resist this is also significant, and perhaps marks no substantial disagreement. So I believe these definitions can stand, at least as parameters of discussion. It is an overall picture of identity which includes most main strands of discourse about it – in modernity and postmodernity, in secular and Christian thinking.

Personal identity and the divine–human analogy

However, simply to define the issues of identity in this way does not settle their validity. This is especially true of personhood. How secure is that in our current state of flux? How can we be sure there *is* any such continuity – and how can we live accordingly?

It is here that a theological basis makes its bid. If God is the ultimate basis of what and who we are, then we should draw from his identity to understand our own. The propriety of this *analogia entis* between divine and human identity is largely beyond dispute, once we admit the propriety of theology at all. Even Karl Barth operated with it when he derived what he calls human personhood from the divine trinitarian personhood.[4] It is an inevitable consequence of any creator–creature relationship, the doctrine of creation in the image of God, and above all the doctrine of incarnation. When God made himself accessible in action he translated himself into human terms. So we shall only know God in the human self, and we shall only know the human self in God. This theological analogy cannot be construed apart from experience, social anthropology, critical reflection, but does not reduce to them. It remains a primary basis for any anthropology which is genuinely theological.

How then does it work? What does it permit us to say about ourselves? What sort of human identity actually emerges from it?

Analogies are formed out of likeness and unlikeness – and it is often easier to begin with areas of unlikeness. One obvious point of unlikeness between divine and human identity has already been indicated. This is the matter of contingency. There is no *ultimate* contingency in God. God's personhood, though relational, is self-sufficient, held within the Trinity. He does not need others external to himself to be himself. Even when aspects of becoming, contingency, change, are construed in God's relations with the world, or even within himself, it is always part of the divine perfection, integrity, 'wholeness'. This is both a moral and ontological truth. It is entailed by the moral perfection and ontological ultimacy which must always belong to God's being as God. It is, precisely, part of the divine identity. But contingency in human identity is a different matter. Theologically, we only exist in any sense by dependence on God. Or else, without God, we only exist by chance. Once brought into being, even our most fundamental and unchanging aspect of identity (our personhood) still only exists by relation to God or others, and is finite. In this sense I agree with McFadyen's wariness with talk of a 'substantial personal core'. It must not be taken as something entirely self-subsistent. Other critical aspects of our identity to do with gender, social role, character, are also radically contingent. As noted already, they are open to profound change or dissolution even within life, changes which may just as easily threaten our identity as fulfil it. Unlike change within God, they are not obviously or inevitably held within some overall state of perfection or completion. Our sometimes shattered sense of selfhood tells us this, quite apart from any a priori theological dogma of fall or sin.

Much the same point can be put in terms of freedom and power. As Barth insisted, God is always free and able to be fully himself in all situations, even when he is construed as a dynamic, changing self (a primary meaning of divine omnipotence). By contrast we are not free to be ourselves in this way. The selves that we are (our actual identity) are not necessarily a true fulfilment of our selfhood (our potential identity). This is not just to do with the sort of potentiality intrinsic to any involvement in time and change which God might share. It refers to a moral or ontological deficiency which means we are not fully ourselves at any stage in the process. We lack the freedom and power always to be truly and fully ourselves. This may be partly our responsibility, individually and collectively. The exercise of our limited, creaturely freedom may have constrained our freedom. The biblical mythology of Adam and Eve, Pauline theology and the common experience of developmental psychology all testify to this possibility. But whatever the origins of our bonds, the fact that we experience some constraint to freedom is evident – and it is a condition radically different from God's.

Another difference derives from the scope of God's relation to the world. Whether this is construed as purposive action in the world or as panentheistic presence, it is the whole world to which God relates. God's identity as creator and redeemer is bound up in this kind of omnipresence, just as much as in omnipotence. Such universal presence and purposes may only be grasped in the particulars of this world, but they relate to all particulars. But our identity cannot be defined like this. No individual, nor the human race collectively, relates in that way to all time and space. The promises of science and pretensions of information technology do not bridge that gap. They expand our knowledge of the sheer multitude of particulars which fill the gap, and add some new kinds of relations with them. But the gap itself remains huge and unbridgeable, both quantitatively and qualitatively.

Such are some of the clearest points of difference. But the positive connections of the analogy are also clear enough.[5] These arise largely out of the points of difference – which is to be expected in any responsible analogical approach to theological method. It naturally expresses meaning about God and the world by a counterpoint of connected meanings, allowing both negative and positive meanings to qualify each other.[6] And it is here that the substance of human identity begins to emerge.

First there is the notion of personhood itself. The fact of our personhood finds warrant in God's. The difference is already clear: our ultimate dependence on God for personhood qualifies it with contingency. But this doesn't diminish the notion of personhood per se. It is subject to the sort of ultimate contingency that belongs to all finite being, but otherwise the perception of human personhood as an enduring, unitary, relational continuum of our being stands as an image of divine being. Just as God is and remains who he is as the one and the same God in time and eternity, so do we (even into eternity). In other words, however we are brought into being and whatever changes we may experience, we do not then become a sequence of different persons, nor do we become something other than persons. Moreover, since this derives from the ultimacy of God, it states both what is the case and what ought to be the case. It will matter, therefore, to live and act on this basis, in relation to ourselves and others. That is how we will be true to our personal identity.

This unitary view of personhood is consistently expressed throughout the Christian theological tradition. It is the presupposition of all biblical narratives. Individuals and peoples are called by God through profound changes in their identity, even given new names, but their essential continuity as persons is guaranteed by the narrative genre itself. As a genre of continuous stories, rather than disconnected scenes, it is always displaying the same person or people, however radical the changes. In the case of the prototypical person of Jesus Christ the story even continues beyond the disjunction of death, and gives hope that the same may be true for others. The unitary person is therefore the presupposition of all salvation history. It is also part of a widespread common-sense disposition. It resonates with almost all experience of selfhood, our own sense of identity, without needing explicit theological warrant. This is not just true for the self-consciousness of Western individualism. Story-telling, with its profound implication for the unitary person, spans the centuries and crosses cultures

As indicated already, this is not uncontested. McFadyen's concerns about the underlying language of substance have been noted. But there is a further critique from the philosopher Derek Parfit which is of quite a different order.[7] For Parfit, enduring personhood does not matter at all. What matters is not that we endure through time or even into eternity: it matters only that (other) persons might exist in the future with the same set of dispositions and intentions as we currently possess. 'We' might be just a temporary bundle of dispositions defined only by its contemporary reality. Merely having concern for the continuity of this bundle (this 'self') does not provide an adequate basis for believing that this continuity is the case, or ought to be the case. Such self-concern might just be a natural egoism which would be better sloughed off, as Buddhists aim to lose possession of their selves.

But Parfit's position is easily refuted. It is not just egoism which drives the instinct for continuity. The instinct is bolstered by more moral and common-sense considerations, quite apart from theological reasons. For instance, if 'I' do not exist in the future in any sense as the same person as I now am, this erodes my sense of responsibility for any action with long-term consequences. I will not own either 'my' past or future. It also fails to provide any basis for valuing other people in relation to their past or future, except in so far as they currently value it for themselves. This has a strangely flattening effect in human relations – and a potentially chilling one if we reduce the significance of the very young or elderly to their present personhood, unrelated to the wider narrative of their lives. There is also a conceptual difficulty in denying our own unity, trying to think of ourselves as a series of disparate persons. Our very capacity for making concepts presupposes an ability to correlate and compare particulars *over a period of time*, requiring the same person as subject of that process. Ordinary common sense confirms the intuition in the most mundane of practices. We all make some self-involving plans for the future, even it is simply to subscribe to insurance plans and pension schemes. We do so, presumably, on the straightforward basis that we think we shall be the same person in the future, at least in some sense.

For more systematic rebuttal of Parfit's position it is the general narrative form of life which counts most. As noted, it is essential to Judaeo-Christian origins – but it is also widespread in other human tradition and experience. Paul Ricoeur presses this point. He is aware that the argument has special theological weight, but he is always concerned to present it on these much wider grounds. The full meaning of personal identity emerges generally through time and narrative, not just the Judaeo-Christian narrative. It is expressed within any context of both change and continuity in which persons ('selfhood', in Ricoeur's terminology) persist with accountable actions and reactions. They do so because it is still *this* person and no other engaged in the plot. The reality of radical change is not denied, nor its capacity to shatter profound aspects of personal identity. Nonetheless, it is still the same person whose identity is being affected. Otherwise we would not even be interested in telling stories about ourselves or other people. Thus:

> even in the most extreme cases of the loss of sameness-identity of the hero, we do not escape the problematic of selfhood. . . . we would not be interested in the drama of dissolution and would not be thrown into perplexity by it, if the non-subject were not still a figure of the subject.[8]

This insistence on continuity is aimed not just at Parfit's analytical speculations but also at extreme postmodern notions of 'person' – which conceive the person to exist only in disconnected moments and unconnected contexts of meaning.

This analysis of Ricoeur can be reinforced by the straightforward observation of 'character' in story-telling. Some of the most intelligent narrative depicts the unitary self, not just through its basic narrative form but in the positive content of its characterizations. The very notion of 'character' is critical here. It can incorporate significant change and development as the self progresses through the story, but it is most compelling when we see it bearing some sort of consistency through these changes. Dickens may be said to fail in this. His characters sometimes act fundamentally (and improbably) out of character. Trollope is a better guide, and George Eliot better still. Whatever the apparent change of attitude and lifestyle, they are shown still to be recognizably themselves in what they have become. This ability to demonstrate a credible but connected development of character is one of the great insights into human identity of a good novelist.[9]

A second point of connection between divine and human is the relational nature of personhood. The relationality which belongs eternally to God's trinitarian being and in God's temporal relation to the world is the ultimate basis for defining the relational nature of human personhood. This trinitarian relationality of God's being does not translate univocally into human being – otherwise the Trinity would reduce either to tritheism or unitarianism. But this does not diminish the significance of relationality per se. Just as God would not be God without relationality, so human being would not be itself in unrelated isolation: individually and collectively our identity is fundamentally relational.

This is a perception about human identity widely discussed in recent theology and anthropology. It is also accepted in recent political philosophy, sociology and psychology.[10] The connection between theology and anthropology in the history of ideas may be very close here: the origin of the very notion of relational personhood has been attributed to the Christian doctrine of the Trinity (though this claim has also been disputed).[11] A powerful case has also been made for an epistemological connection. Because both God and humanity are essentially relational, we can only know God in personal relation to him, by participation in the trinitarian reality of mutual (loving) relations. The ontology behind this is again given persuasive expression by Ricoeur in terms of narrative. Narrative is the matrix within which the self is revealed as essentially relational, as well as unitary. Within the structure of a story the self always unfolds in relation to others (and, for Ricoeur, in relation to itself: there is also an internal relatedness of self to its own body and 'conscience').[12] So narrative clearly signals a relational and dynamic ontology of personhood, for human as for divine identity. It is an ontology of personal being which has little to do with the abstract, static, isolated individual of the Enlightenment legacy.

This is particularly important for the discussion of this

book. It underlines change itself as a point of connection with the divine identity, as well as a point of difference. It clearly presents change as something which contributes to the potential fulfilment of human identity, not just threatens it. This is a direct implication of a relational and unitary notion of personhood. An isolated notion of the person could fulfil her individual identity without change: this is as true of the disconnected postmodern person as it is for the classic Cartesian ego of modernism. But an essentially related and unitary person cannot be truly himself in isolation from the change entailed by his connectedness with other people and situations through the sequence of time.

Freedom is another point of connection. Its extent is arguable, and it is obviously different from God's. It is circumscribed by our finitude, contingency, failings. But it must still exist in some form for personal relations with God or others. It is integral to our status as creatures in *imago dei*, and in the *analogia entis* with God. If there is no sense in which we can contribute or co-operate in becoming ourselves, then the selfhood that belongs to us loses all meaning within that analogy. What we experience would not be selfhood but the delusions of a puppet of the creator. A qualified freedom must therefore belong to human identity. This affects the meaning of character, disposition, and the sense of call or vocation. They matter as aspects of human personal identity in a different way to biologically determined aspects because they bear traces of individual or collective choice and assent. In this sense they share in a key aspect of divine identity – the God who is entirely free to be himself. This is the presupposition of almost all Judaeo-Christian narrative and doctrine, except in its extreme fringes of predestinarianism. In wider thought it is a matter of philosophical debate, fuelled increasingly by the determinism of socio-biological anthropologies. But some sense of freedom and responsibility will always remain. It is utterly essential to common-sense presuppositions of practical living. We cannot live without it.

Particularity also connects us to God, in spite of profound differences. Prima facie it seems to speak only of finitude and limitation, not of God at all. Being a particular person is to be bound to particular space and time and identified with a particular gender, race, personality. It is precisely the kind of limitation we expect to be negated in the meaning of God, who is not just *a* particular person and whose access to time and space cannot be restricted to any particular part of it. That is part of the meaning of divine omnipresence and omnipotence. However, what God transcends she also includes. As we saw, the double negative of the apophatic way allows this affirmation. So it is equally part of the meaning of omnipotence to *be* particular, as well as to relate to all particulars and transcend them. This is true of the meaning of God in himself, the radical meaning of differentiated persons within the Trinity which must not be reduced to monism.[13] It is also true of God's pivotal action of self-expression in the world in the Incarnation. The particularity of Jesus of Nazareth in history, geography, ethnicity, gender is not a scandal to the divine identity but an essential part of it. It is, in fact, the critical means by which the transcendent God can then relate effectively (and savingly) to all particulars *as* particulars.[14]

This provides an endorsement of our particularity. It is not a prison to break out of but the prism through which we too relate most effectively to other particulars in the world. We fulfil our personal identity as people of particular background and particular calling. This is clear in the Judaeo-Christian narratives. God meets, calls and shapes particular individuals and nations chiefly by acting and addressing them within their particular social context, not through timeless Socratic truths.[15] And when there is some call to change, this is always from one particular place, relationship, community, to another, never to a universal or abstract identity. It has been the massive achievement of Alasdair MacIntyre to show how this resonates with the general needs of a 'virtuous' human society. His critique of the Enlightenment project is precisely that abstract universals fail to cement community effectively and lead to the moral and social disintegration of postmodernity. That is why there is such an urgent need to rediscover the value of particular narrative traditions. Both his critique of the

Enlightenment and his preferred solution have received criticism, but the overall analysis remains compelling.[16]

This does not endorse disconnected particularity. The extreme postmodern celebration of 'difference' absolutizes disconnectedness with no warrant in logic or experience. That leads inexorably to chaos and irresponsibility. It is the complete opposite of an endorsement of particularity through which connections are more truthfully made. So this celebration of particularity which fulfils identity is not the retreat to tribalism. Instead, it is the sort of blessing of Abraham which will make him a blessing to others; it is the sort of incarnation in Christ which will enable God, through him, to reconcile *all* things; it is the sort of affirmation of the racially denigrated which will empower them to love rather than withdraw; it is the sort of cultivation of institutional or national identities which will motivate wider responsibilities rather than self-preoccupation.

Such is an outline of human identity which emerges from a theological basis. It is unitary and enduring, but also incorporates the full texture of temporality, change, becoming, potential. It is particular but also relational, so it always involves purposes or callings beyond itself. It means we cannot find our true personal identity in any one isolated moment of time or within any isolated sense of self: it will always require some sort of wider narrative for its fulfilment. All this derives directly from Christian theology, but finds ready resonance in many empirical anthropologies and common-sense perceptions. It positions a Christian view of personal identity between – or beyond – both modernity and postmodernity. It is neither the abstract and isolated individual of the former nor the transient and disconnected bundle of relations of the latter.

Fulfilling human identity: love and faithfulness

The central question can now be put again. Given this kind of identity, how do we live best? What specific moral substance of character, dispositions, and what kind of actions, fulfil this sort of identity? What particular directions are given by such theological foundations – and how do they relate beyond the theological tradition? How does this relate to Royce's call to loyalty?

Again it is love, not loyalty, which presents itself as the most obvious response to begin with. Its significance has been well recognized at various stages of historical moral theology, and particularly in recent discussion. As with divine love, theological analysis of human love has been exhaustive and the literature extensive.[17] The love at the heart of divine identity and being calls for answering love from human being and naturally fulfils this sort of identity. The love of biblical narrative is generous and enduring but also creative, dynamic and responsive, able to incorporate change. It is particular but not exclusive; it is to be practised not just with friends but with neighbours, even enemies. The self-giving of love is so radical that it can be described as 'losing self', but it is not the obliteration of all meanings of identity because 'he who loses himself will also find it'. In other words, it is a love which presupposes a free, recognizable, relational self which has something to give to the other; it presupposes a self which remains itself in order for love itself to remain. In this way the narrative of love incorporates change and even death (sacrifice) within personal identity, but still implies the persistence of personhood. This is all part of the meaning of love at the heart of Christian ethics. It is an undisputed centre of biblical teaching and narrative, given explicit endorsement in Christ's 'greatest commandment' of the Gospels and Paul's eulogy to love as the 'highest gift' in 1 Corinthians: without love we are 'nothing', we have no identity; with love we have all that matters.

Aspects of this kind of love also feature in secular anthropologies – particularly its basic shape as a relational ethic which requires selfhood (even self-esteem) to persist even in radical concern for the other. This is a fundamental aspect of much contemporary psychology. It is a concern of feminist thought, anxious to redeem love from mere submission. It also arises, as might be expected, from more general narrative accounts of the self. Ricoeur is especially insistent that what he calls benevolence is integrally related to self-esteem; the ethical primacy of the 'other' has to include a real self with which to recognize the other and respond. He characteristically links this with a biblical command ('love your neighbour as yourself') but also seeks to derive it from much wider discussion.[18]

All this is widely and rightly accepted. But it still raises the same question which had to be asked of divine love and divine identity. Can the *generality* of love deliver its full meaning, and fulfil the full meaning of human identity? What specific forms does love take – *particularly in relation to time and change*? This again raises the question of faithfulness as a defining feature of love and of human identity. Since faithfulness is so significant for divine identity through time and change, we might expect it to function in the same way for human identity. It needs to be investigated.

5

THE CALL TO HUMAN
FAITHFULNESS

Biblical narratives and their traditions

A theological investigation of human faithfulness must begin
with the same biblical narratives where divine faithfulness is
celebrated. There divine faithfulness first invites the response
of trust. But it also clearly seeks an answering response of
human faithfulness – to God and others. It is an essential
human correlate within covenant theology. In one way or
another human faithfulness is always required.[1] This is imme-
diately apparent from the narratives themselves and the traditions they have generated. It is displayed, like God's, as a
critical and timeful mode of being, a vital constituent of our
identity both corporate and personal.

In the first case, the people of Israel are called to be faithful
to the one God, over against all other gods. In the histories of
the patriarchs, the exodus, the exile, they are called to keep
faith through time, change, judgement, suffering and perplexity. The existential form of struggling with faithfulness is a
main theme of the Psalms and the Book of Job. The challenge
to maintain this faithfulness is a theme of the prophets. In the
New Testament faithfulness to Christ is the presupposition of
discipleship in the Gospel narratives. Peter is shaped in his
identity as disciple and key apostle for the Church precisely
through the process of learning faithfulness through failure.
Likewise in the Pauline epistles, it is a frequent exhortation
both to individuals and churches to 'continue steadfast in the

faith, without shifting from the hope promised by the Gospel': it is an essential outworking of Christian identity as a 'reconciled' person.[2] In the apocalypse an extraordinary array of imagery is ordered to this central aim: keeping the churches faithful to their calling through times of persecution. It is a critical part of fulfilling the identity of the Church.

All this is a call of religious faithfulness to God. The call of ethical faithfulness to others or to institutions is less explicit, but still present. It is implicit in the dominical command to 'love one another as I have loved you':[3] i.e. through the timeful process of teaching, healing, discipling, and the sort of commitment conveyed by his death and resurrection. It is implied in the teachings of the Sermon on the Mount. The command to forgive not once but seven times seven implies persistence and process. The beatitude promised to those who 'hunger and thirst after righteousness' suggests a faithful struggle through time.[4] What is promised as a result is, specifically, to do with fulfilling identity: a condition of being 'filled'. Faithfulness is also evident in Paul's exposition of the highest gift: the love which means 'bearing all things, believing all things, hoping all things, enduring all things'.[5] This is an essentially timeful hermeneutic of love, requiring faithfulness. The context here is the relation of members of the Church to one another.

What social form does this call to faithfulness take? Marriage is one example. This is evident in the use of covenant concepts to describe marriage, in both Old and New Testaments. Covenant relationship as moral agreement 'signifying . . . commitment, which includes both promises and obligations . . . which has the quality of reliability and durability'[6] is strongly implied in the seminal text of Genesis which Jesus endorses in Mark's Gospel.[7] To 'cleave' to a wife and become one flesh which 'no one should separate' sets a normative structure for marriage in which faithfulness is essential. The prophets Hosea, Jeremiah, Ezekiel, Deutero-Isaiah also refer to marriage in the context of covenant. They use a marital metaphor in their primary task of recalling Israel to its covenant relationship with God. This is largely in the context of broken relationships, and the positive meaning for marriage is only implicit as the backdrop of the metaphor. But the positive use of the metaphor is explicit enough in the New Testament Letter to the Ephesians. Although the word covenant does not occur, the pairing of husband–wife and Christ–Church relationships is clearly intended as a covenantal analogy. It is applied directly to husbands and wives. It also expresses the significance of this relationship for personal identity. Like the notion of 'one flesh', this (faithful) covenantal relationship conveys something mutually constitutive for the identity of the partners: 'in loving a wife a man loves *himself*'.[8]

The appropriation of these biblical metaphors within Christian tradition has been varied. The more grudging strands of Pauline teaching about marriage, the influence of asceticism and platonic dualism, and recent feminism have all had their effect. The status of marriage itself has oscillated between the powerful early critiques of Gregory of Nyssa and John Chrysostom, twelfth-century high sacramentalism (literally,'pledge of fidelity'), the Calvinist recovery of covenantal concepts, and radical deconstruction of its patriarchal and oppressive aspects. Understanding of the limits to marriage faithfulness has also varied. Divorce, indissolubility, annulment, all feature – however controversially – within the Christian tradition as a whole. But none of it affects the basic claim that faithfulness, in some sense, is critical for defining the meaning of love in marriage.

Kinship is another social sphere for fidelity – though it is more equivocal. The Old Testament patriarchal stories imply some exemplary, quasi-covenantal models of faithfulness within family life: although tricked by Joseph, Isaac still gives him his blessing; although betrayed by his brothers, Joseph does not finally disown them. However, because the characters in these stories serve representative and typological purposes in a wider story about Israel, their ethical implications are not straightforward. The narratives are more aetiological legends about the formation of a people than moral tales about individual characters. The Deuteronomic law offers an easier genre of literature to interpret. Its injunction to honour father and mother, its high regard for first-born male children in the processes of inheritance, preferential treatment to brothers in the remarriage of a widow, all express some sort of loyalty in kinship. But here too there are significant qualifications: in particular this 'ethical' loyalty is always strictly subordinate to religious faithfulness; if any relation entices another to religious apostasy the commitment is abruptly ended.[9] The prophets who rail generally against the breakdown of interpersonal loyalty and responsibility as a symptom of wider covenant unfaithfulness are more convincing exponents of the significance of kinship ties. However, it is noteworthy how much of this concern is directed towards orphans and widows. These are to be supported by virtue of their generic kinship with the tribe rather than their specific kinship within a family unit. In the New Testament the picture is not dissimilar. There is Jesus' long-term provision for his mother at his death, and Mary's faithfulness to her son, in spite of his apparent indifference on occasions. This could be construed normatively. There are the household codes of the epistles which enjoin obedience and mutual respect between family members – an implicit call to faithfulness. On the other hand these kinship loyalties are also relativized by a higher loyalty to the Kingdom of God: 'my mother and my brothers are those who do the will of my heavenly father'; sometimes we may have to '*leave* brother or sisters or mother or father or children for the sake of the Gospel'.[10] So there are mixed signals here. Nonetheless, the sphere of kinship clearly features. It can witness to the Kingdom even if is not the Kingdom itself.[11] It cannot be ignored.

Subsequent reflection on these foundations has taken place, but it is fairly limited. Christian tradition has largely assumed that kinship has some significance and that loyalty will play some role. But it has varied in its evaluation. The Reformation recovery of 'ordinary life' as a high calling – over against the elitism of special religious vocations – specifically entailed valuing kinship and fulfilling its commitments.[12] On the other hand, particular religious vocation has often been accepted as

a call to qualify or overturn the commitment. This has been a
driving force behind both monastic ideals and evangelical
missionary endeavour. Critiques of kinship commitment have
also been offered in the feminist hermeneutic of suspicion: as
with marriage, the call to kinship loyalty can easily mask a
manipulative exercise of power. It is ripe for deconstruction.
Nonetheless, kinship per se still features in the tradition. It
remains a social context for exercising faithfulness. And it
is bound to remain, not least because it relates to such
fundamental connections between people. Because we are
embodied persons our blood relations will always create a
recognition of self in the other in a unique way. So the fact that
it is not particularly dominant in the biblical narratives and
Christian tradition may simply be a consequence of its
obvious importance: it was too powerful and widespread an
assumption of social life and natural law to warrant more
explicit justification. How we exercise faithfulness within
kinship structures will therefore remain significant.

Much the same can be said of the two other major social
spheres for the call to faithfulness in the biblical traditions.
Church and state (religion and nation) command loyalty,
sometimes inseparably – but again, equivocally. In the Old
Testament history of Israel the connection between tribe,
nation, temple and monarchy is a complex and shifting set of
relations, affected by war, exile, and the religious-moral state
of both leaders and people. The identification of God himself
with each or all of these is similarly varied. There are periods
of close identification and of significant separation. An
anointed king can embody both the nation and the will of
Yahweh, but can also be the reason for the nation's downfall
and God's wrath.[13] The temple can be a unique place of God's
presence and the gateway to heaven, or else the subject of
radical prophetic critique in which the obligations of covenant
are set against the temple rather than fulfilled in it.[14]
Nonetheless, the identity of Israel is still bound up with these
institutions, even when they are corrupt. So it is not surprising
that people's belonging to them generates a call to faithfulness. It is cast in various forms. A key form of expressing

faithfulness to 'nation' is the regular observance of Passover. The identity of the people of Israel is affirmed and reaffirmed in this remembrance and repetition of the constitutive events of exodus, just as it involves keeping the law which also constituted their identity. Similarly, faithfulness to the temple is structured in the regular observance of ceremony, festival and sacrifice. These are all essentially temporal activities, seeking to transcend time by bringing either past or future events into the liturgical present, by the (faithful) repetition of these activities through time. The expression of loyalty to the monarchy of the Davidic line is less specific, but it is a correlate of God's covenant to David 'and his house for ever'. This promise to David is to be 'an instruction for the people' as well.[15] When the monarchy disintegrates, faithfulness to it is structured through the persistence of messianic hope, to be fulfilled eventually by David's heir.

In the New Testament the Church is mostly at a primitive pre-institutional stage, not yet identified with any state. Faithfulness to it as 'the body of Christ', whatever its failings, is therefore more straightforward. Paul's own example is evident throughout his letters, but especially in Corinthians and Galatians. He deliberately displays the history of his own sufferings, struggles, journeys, deepest longings, as evidence of his total commitment through time to planting and building up church communities. His teaching is meant to do likewise. Church members are to prize most those gifts which build up the church, and to 'devote themselves to the service of the saints . . . to put themselves at the service of everyone who works and toils with them'.[16] It is clearly a *process* of faithful belonging envisaged here, not just a status. The charge levelled against Paul that this is merely manipulative rhetoric, incidentally, need not detain us. To the extent that it sticks, it calls into question only the means not the ends of his call to faithfulness. The same point holds for the Epistle to the Ephesians, where its high doctrine of the Church elicits a similarly persuasive personal confession of faithfulness to it. The writer explains how he is 'completing in his flesh what is lacking in Christ's afflictions for the sake of his body, that is the church'.[17] It is, again, a belonging to the Church textured by struggle, suffering, goal-seeking, experienced through a process of time. The more general terms of Pauline theology make the same point more simply: the critical status for human identity of *being* in Christ is also, inseparably, a dynamic *following* of Christ.

The state in the New Testament also commands some loyalty – though naturally there is more ambivalence about it. It is God-ordained in the Pauline view of Romans and Thessalonians, with the task of maintaining order and holding back chaos. But it also has the potential for totalitarianism, usurping its ordained role, becoming the beast of Revelation which persecutes the Church. Jesus' own attitude to it depicted in the Gospels appears to straddle both possibilities. This is summarized in the gnomic saying about taxes: some things belong to Caesar, some things belong to God.[18] Nonetheless, a call to belong with some loyalty, however qualified, is still stated. Proper dues must be paid. In the pastoral Epistle to Timothy when the institution of the Church was developing with longer-term responsibilities to the world around it, loyalty to state rulers is taken further. It will involve prayer over time, directed for a lifetime of 'peaceable life'.[19]

This basic biblical call for a faithful belonging – to both Church and state – has had to negotiate huge changes in circumstance and social context. The Constantinian settlement, the religious–social structures of medieval Christendom, Reformation and schism, secularization, war, allegations of church collusion in oppressive twentieth-century ideologies, have all left their mark on the meaning of belonging and the kind of loyalty that is appropriate. Nonetheless, as with marriage and kinship, both these social spheres have remained areas of concern (joined, as we shall see, by other areas of social practice now emerging as more significant). They all matter for human identity and call for some form of faithfulness

In such ways the biblical traditions clearly set an agenda for faithful living. 'Faithfulness' of some kind is a critical ingredient in the narratives both for individual and social life. It is confirmed as a critical process through time, closely bound up with matters of both individual and corporate identity. It takes different forms in varying social contexts, but the imperative to realize it in some way is incontrovertible.

Faithfulness, Christian ethics, and the importance of character

Can the development of faithful Christian living in these (and other) areas be charted in more detail? To do this in a substantive way would be a huge task. It constitutes much of the content of Christian ethics down the centuries. It would mean a theological review of the role of faithfulness in all areas of human living from patristic to postmodern times. That is not for this book. However, there is another way of assessing the developing significance of the call to faithfulness. It can be demonstrated effectively by a summary of Christian ethical theory, rather than content. The point of this is to show what framework of ethical thought is particularly hospitable to notions like 'faithfulness' and the formation of faithful character. In particular, it will show whether the prevailing trend in ethical theory demands it. And if this is the case faithfulness will have been placed even more decisively at the centre of the ethical map.

A summary of Christian ethical theory means chiefly a survey of the way Christian reflection has taken its biblical traditions into different kinds of interpretative frameworks. It entails some engagement with secular philosophical traditions of interpretation and application. The reasons are obvious. God's decisive address in Christ and the whole biblical witness, and his address to us now, are both historicized. This means there is always a passage of time and change to connect his 'total' address to us: it has to span both biblical and contemporary worlds, opening up huge hermeneutical space. Within this space the Christian ethicist is bound to engage with all kinds of human experience and reflection, simply because *all* human being and identity is ultimately determined and addressed by the one creator God. Such hermeneutical engagement with the full range of experience is therefore integral to the Christian task of ethics, not extra to it. This is even true of dogmatic theological ethics based on positivist views of revelation. Even Barth says that theological ethics must 'in its very loyalty to it [i.e. its own task] . . . establish a continuous relationship of its thinking and speaking with the human ethical problem *as a whole*'.[20] This story of these 'continuous relationships' therefore lies at the heart of any review of ethical theory. It is a familiar story, but bears repeating to show the background from which its most recent trends have emerged.

The earliest influence was neo-platonic. This is found in Augustine and amongst many others. By assimilating a metaphysical form of 'the Good' with God, and identifying the vision of this God with the fulfilment of the soul, Christian theology provided a widely communicable philosophical–religious structure for ethical priorities to emerge. However, these depended largely on metaphysical and moral dualisms between this world and God, soul and body, which have not wedded well with Judaeo-Christian ethics. So other interpretative frameworks were sought – and the alliance between Aristotelian and classic Thomist moral theology was the next major example. In the premodern period it articulated a compelling anthropology. The 'virtuous' person was one responsible for acting within an essentially purposive world in fundamental harmony with her own purposive human nature. But these metaphysics were then undermined by the rise of rational scientific enquiry. This challenged the natural purposiveness of the world – which seemed neither verifiable, reliable, or self-evident.

This in turn led rationalism to offer its own tools for the ethicist. It could provide a rational and empirical basis for ethics which would determine right action by weighing observable consequences. This is the essence of utilitarianism, which based right action on one foundational rule: a sophisticated calculation of maximizing benefits of happiness for the largest number of people. Its Christian counterpart has been mentioned earlier: Joseph Fletcher's situation ethics is a calculation of how to maximize the specific benefits of 'love'; right action is determined by the one rule only, which is to do the most loving thing in the present, given, situation. The Kantian alternative sought the foundational rule instead in the good will rather than the calculation of consequences. This good will is determined by its universal application: i.e. what is right is what I would will for all, not just for myself. This had its Christian alliance in the appropriation of the golden rule: 'do unto others only what you would have done to yourself'. Karl Barth's 'occasionalist' ethics, though not rationalist, has also echoed aspects of both situationism and Kant. God's address comes afresh and individually to all in each moment, undetermined by any source other than the authority of his own revealed will.

But here too the alliance has been provisional. All these varieties of rationally (or revelationally) based ethics have had their flaws. Empirical notions of 'happiness', even if they could be reliably calculated, failed to satisfy the full moral texture of human fulfilment. An overriding appeal to consequences pushed the basis of decision-making into an unknown future, a mere potentiality. Equally, decisions made to meet the demands of love just in the present situation atomized the present and failed to take adequate account of past and future continuities. In this way it emasculates the meaning of human identity. Rational ethics has tended to separate actions from the whole self. It has shifted attention onto the decision-making of rational, abstract individuals, and away from the formation of people as relational characters within a wider community, story, tradition. Eventually, when reason itself came to be treated with such suspicion in the dawn of the deconstructive era, ethics simply fragmented into mere preference or 'emotivism'. Some Christian feminist ethics have welcomed the negative, deconstructive aspect of this last move. It has unmasked patriarchal power games hiding behind the abstracting and universalizing tendencies of rational ethics, the flattening of particularities in human being into a uniformly male mould. But it is one thing to deconstruct. It is another to provide positive ethics – and so most theological ethics are still left looking elsewhere for a new partner.

The most recent chapter of the story attempts some reconstruction. With Heidegger in the background, then Gadamer, and especially under MacIntyre's influence, the tide has turned back to the continuities of tradition and community. Within a narrative tradition which has dynamic but recognized 'practices' of behaviour, a form of moral rationality emerges which does not depend on static or outmoded metaphysics, nor does it claim the sort of abstract universalizability of Enlightenment reason. But it does offer something widely authoritative and communicable, at least within that tradition (and its success in those terms can then be a basis for a genuinely communicative dialogue between traditions). As such it entails a profoundly relational view of human identity. Persons are formed, given character and fulfilled only within a community bearing such a narrative tradition. The community itself is formed and given its character over the period of time that any dynamic tradition requires. Persons therefore act most truly to themselves when they act out of this individual and collective character. The shift in ethical concern is away from isolated acts and decisions and back to the character of the whole person, construed as essentially relational and formed as *a continuous subject through time*.

This has provided another framework for Christian ethical thought, a new partner to work with.[21] The revival of reformulated Aristotelian-Thomist theories of virtue is one aspect of it.[22] The radical ethics and ecclesiology of Stanley Hauerwas are a particular outworking of it.[23] Hauerwas's project is itself a shifting and sometimes disparate enterprise, but there are some pivotal and recurring themes, and they clearly owe much to MacIntyre's overall thesis. The community of the Church, with its distinctive practices of liturgical worship and rehearsing biblical narrative, generates a people with distinctive character and dispositions. For example, acting out of those practices and character will lead us to trust more in the value of the future, as well as the present, because it is *God's* future. Children, therefore, are to be specially valued as signs of trust in God's future: abortion generally becomes lack of faith. It will also mean that all coercion is forbidden, because that would deny God's way of moving forward to the future: so war too is lack of faith. However, the chief point is this. These dispositions have not been adopted by rational analysis of cost-benefits, nor by weighing up consequences, nor even by immediate divine guidance or individual intuition. They cannot be communicated authoritatively on any of those grounds. Their 'rationality' emerges only and precisely by belonging to the narrative tradition and practices of the Church. The moral self has taken up these attitudes not because she has faced a series of particular decisions but because he is a continuously formed character. For Hauerwas this is the only condition in which we can live truthfully through situations of moral conflict and tragedy. These defy moral resolution by discrete acts or decisions. Only a character formed within this narrative community can remain moral through these tragedies of life which do not permit particular moral solutions.[24]

The sectarian tendencies of this ecclesiology, and its retreat from rational apologetics, have been heavily criticized (though also defended).[25] The ethical stance which emerges from it on specific issues like abortion and pacifism is often controversial. Nonetheless, it represents a very significant attempt in recent Christian ethics to engage with current frameworks of thought. In particular, it engages with both major strands of thought about human identity. That is, it incorporates the unitary, enduring self of Christian narrative (and modernism) which undergirds the persistence and connections of character over time. But it also assumes the relational, social and changing self of Christian narrative (and current anthropology) which provides the changing dynamic of this character. In other words, it takes account of modernity and postmodernity, but positions the meaning of Christian personal identity beyond both. It illustrates a vital trajectory which all contemporary Christian ethical theory must take, whatever the merits of its particular outworking in Hauerwas.

So here we reach the nub of this account. Here is a

significant trend in contemporary Christian ethics which is also most obviously an ethic of faithfulness. Faithfulness is bound to be a key virtue in the tradition-formed character of this kind of ethical framework. The capacity to persist through time and change in the dynamic but connected way demanded by the practices of a narrative tradition is precisely the meaning of faithfulness. Royce saw this with loyalty: 'training' a character over time is integral to real virtue and fulfilled identity. It is how such identity realizes itself and becomes a truly moral identity. It inhabits, incorporates and responds to time and change, but without ceasing to be itself in its overall purpose of love. So whatever particular personal and social issues we face we are most likely to face them best in the exercise of some form of faithfulness. In short, the notion of faithfulness which claims us first from the identity of God, then from specific religious and ethical demands in the biblical traditions, also pushes its way convincingly into the heart of current ethical theory. Once again faithfulness calls for, and deserves, our attention.

6

A CONTEMPORARY CONTEXT: CHANGE, IDENTITY AND THE PROBLEM OF TIME

Theology offers a particular understanding of human identity. It suggests that faithfulness is a key notion for fulfilling that identity through time and change. The ultimate basis for this lies in the identity of God. The faithfulness which binds God to himself and to us also binds us to ourselves and others. This states the case so far, and invites a theological agenda in which faithfulness should always feature because it is an internal priority. But of course a theological agenda must not just be self-determined: it must always be responsive to the public world. A crying need in contemporary culture will always be another reason for a theological priority. It will point to the place where a spiritual battle must be especially focused. Luther's warning is stark: 'If I profess with the loudest voice and clearest exposition every portion of the truth of God except precisely that little point which the world and devil are at the moment attacking . . . I am not confessing Christ.' In other words we must enter the fray where the battle is currently raging. It is the very essence of discipleship.

The nature of the contemporary social and intellectual battlefield was outlined in the introduction. Change is rapid and directionless. No overarching traditions or metanarratives command sufficient credibility to interpret or guide it. It is a situation where the self and society easily disintegrate, and personal identity becomes an inevitable casualty. This is the context of the spiritual battles of our time – and it is precisely in this context that faithfulness becomes such a compelling response. Although the case for this so far has been largely theological, it clearly resonates far more widely. It naturally presents itself as an icon to be rediscovered: an instrument of healing, for self and society. 'Fidelity [gives] unity to lives that otherwise splinter', wrote Milan Kundera; 'To have roots' and 'participation in the life of a community which preserves . . . treasures of the past and expectations for the future' is a 'fundamental need of the soul', wrote Simone Weil.[1] Both the diagnosis and the treatment echo Royce in his earlier perceptions of social and moral battle.

The problem of time

More now needs to be said about this context. In general it may be described as a deconstruction of traditions with fragmenting consequences for the self and the profound need for faithfulness. But the experience of disintegration which underlies all this invites further analysis. In particular, a disintegrated self suggests more attention needs to be paid to the specific question of *time*.

Time, after all, has always been experienced as a fundamental problem of a disintegrated self. 'I am divided between time gone by and time to come', says Augustine in the *Confessions*. Hamlet is torn apart because 'time is out of joint'. Heidegger repeatedly and explicitly describes the effect of time as 'fragmenting' the self because we fail to integrate our past, present and future.[2] It is not hard to see why. The past seems irretrievable, except through (unreliable) memory, so the guilt, regret and nostalgia with which we inhabit it seems impossible to resolve. The future is unknowable except through (unreliable) imagination, so the fear and fantasy with which we inhabit that also seems beyond resolution. The present is all we have but it is 'specious': it slips away from us into both past and future without having any real existence of its own.

There has been a long tradition of philosophical–theological concern to deal with the problem of time. In addition to

Augustine and Heidegger there are major discussions in Plato, Boethius, Aquinas, Barth, Ricoeur, and so on: a continuing and extensive dialogue of theology with philosophy, science and literature.[3] The particularly difficult period of late modernity has generated its own crop of major discussions, not only in Heidegger and Ricoeur, but also through the literature of Proust, Eliot, Joyce and more recent postmodern novelists. I do not intend to review the whole of this debate, which relates to a very wide range of social and philosophical contexts. But I will focus on the current role that our experience of time is playing in our sense of self – and what that implies for the healing of the self.

Our current experience of time is not easily characterized. Prima facie it might seem that we should have fewer problems with it in late modernity, at least conceptually. For instance, if we can construe it according to the theory of special relativity this could ease the sting of its passing. A notion of space–time as a simultaneous continuum in which all time is laid out like landscape (a 'timescape') suggests that the ultimate reality of time is very different from our broken experience of it. It is a conception of an ultimate connectedness or integration of all time. If this begins to reshape our experience, it ought to satisfy, even to heal.

But it is not as easy as that. This sort of continuum suggests a static sort of connectedness, hardly a satisfactory kind of integration. Also, we only know this concept provisionally. It only seems to work in some areas of physics, and awaits integration with quantum theory, which may tell a different story about time. In any case, the mere concept itself will not necessarily transform experience: we still live in a broken *sense* of time. So it offers no firm assurance either in its grasp on reality or its potential to heal experience. The best it can do is help model some theological concepts of eternity to help bolster faith – but even this has limited value when God's eternity has to be construed more dynamically.

In fact our experience of time is much more likely to be shaped by other factors: not scientific theory but wider metaphysical views (if we have any) embodied in actual social relations and practices. This is the way the Christian meta-narrative certainly *used* to affect our sense of time. Within an overall story of divine judgement, forgiveness and redemption, the past could be erased or reconfigured. An eschatological story of divine power over the future could in principle deal with its fears and correct its fantasies. A community which carried these stories faithfully from one generation to another and embodied them in its liturgical and social practices could then, to some extent, transform this 'theory' into practice. As we saw, this was part of the meaning of Israel's liturgy of passover, carried forward in the Christian Eucharist. In such a community time would not seem arbitrarily broken: it could all be integrated within the eternity of God. The liturgical and social relations of the community of faith would be the plausibility structure which transformed experience to match the theology.

But of course much of this is lost if we have passed beyond this sort of metanarrative, as most have in the late-postmodern period. So our experience of time will be shaped instead by the shifting, unconnected flux of relations and roles which characterize this period. And this is bound to intensify the 'natural' brokenness of time, rather than heal it. This is just what we find in most observations about time of this period. In the literary expressions of it there is a variety of approach, but a common concern. In Proust there is the explicit search for lost time. In the so-called stream of consciousness technique there is recognition of disintegrated time. It is an attempt to overcome the disruption between inner and outer worlds of time, 'private' and 'public' time. Joyce attempts to escape the passing of time by experimenting with repetitive themes, complex neologisms and a cyclical structure: the purpose is to let narrative and meaning flow back into itself in overlapping layers, rather than pursue a single ordered direction. The particular concern of more recent novelists is to leave meaning *open*, avoiding all 'closure'. This is another symptom of the terror of time: we dare not seal anything, because then there is no going back and no going forward.

T. S. Eliot is the most telling poet of time.[4] At the point when he is personally travelling in the reverse direction to society – into Christian faith, rather than away from it – he is most clear-eyed about the condition of transition. He sees all too vividly what is being lost around him which he must rediscover. 'The Love Song of J. Alfred Prufrock' and *The Waste Land* express the banality, meaninglessness, and terror of time which is unconnected and unreconciled to past or future:

> In a minute there is time
> For decisions and revisions which a minute will reverse.
>   ('Prufrock')

> . . . I will show you something different from either
> Your shadow at morning striding behind you
> Or your shadow at evening rising to meet you;
> I will show you fear in a handful of dust. (*The Waste Land*)

In *Ash Wednesday*, shortly after his point of conversion, he explores the difficulty of effectively reconciling past to present in the act of penitence: he is acutely aware of the fragmentation of his own personality between past, present and future. *The Four Quartets* then convey a resolution through appeal to some sort of timeless moment which shows how the end and beginning *can* be brought together – but in a new light, not simply as a vain repetition or cycle of time. Thus:

> . . . the end of all our exploring
> Will be to arrive where we started
> And know the place for the first time. ('Little Gidding').

But even here the resolution is hard won against the backdrop of powerful images of disconnected time, words, and events, which he sees so clearly. Words and traditions 'slip, slide, perish' into the past, and need to be recovered into the new context of the present before we can move safely into the future ('Burnt Norton'). For: 'A people without history [i.e. connected, integrated time]/ Is not redeemed from time' ('Little Gidding'). That is why 'only through time time is conquered' ('Burnt Norton'). The nature of Eliot's resolution – his 'timeless moment' – will repay further attention. For the moment it is the analysis of the problem of time, and its particular intensity in this period, which is notable.

Contributions from philosophy paint a similar picture. Heidegger's preoccupation with time, especially the personal fragmentation of being in time, has already been noted. It is important to him because his whole philosophy of the self is predicated on our being in time. Our personal identity is essentially temporal: we only have our being by being situated in time, historical, 'being-there' (*Dasein*). As such, fragmentation must necessarily be overcome. But the means Heidegger proposes displays the measure of disintegration to be dealt with. Being 'situated' means we must draw all self-understanding out of our immediate, present, existential awareness. Out of this we can orientate ourselves towards the future by being aware of possibilities – but from this same awareness we also know that death is the overarching future which constrains all these possibilities and ends time. This provides a kind of integration, but only by drawing the limits of the future wholly out of present existence and its mortality. In the end this imprisons us again in our experience of temporality rather than overcoming the pain of it. Ricoeur's preoccupation with time is also notable. He moves on from Heidegger in key matters. His horizons for human possibilities go beyond death to eternity.[5] His project to fully understand our personal identity goes beyond the resources of immediate self-awareness: crucially he wants us to understand ourselves, as we have seen, through the process of narrative in which we see ourselves as accountable through a whole ordered process of time, change and relationships. But again, the backdrop to his whole proposal is precisely the *problematic* of time: time in contemporary experience is a problem to the self; it is a matter to be 'reconfigured'. The question is, how can this be done?

Reconfiguring time

Reconfiguring time is a beguiling phrase. It suggests itself as a
necessary and fundamental process of finding or healing our
selves. But what it means, and how it comes about, is harder to
express convincingly. Prima facie it might sound like a total
re-ordering of the flow and direction of time, as if by changing
our interpretation of time we change the *whole* meaning of it.
This would be the far point of non-realism, Kantian logic
taken to the extreme. It would mean there is no 'outside' to our
existence, and our interpretation or experience of it is the only
truth there is. This is the position adopted by Don Cupitt. The
perception of the moment constitutes all there is, which,
inseparably, constitutes the whole meaning of the self. The
whole meaning of time and self coincide in the present, and
this instant of 'eternity' therefore combines all subjective
and 'objective' meaning.[6] With this realization time can be
radically reconfigured because we can (re-)create all its meaning in such moments. But of course there are all sorts of
reasons to dispute this sort of position. Cupitt misreads Kant,
fails to see common-sense counter-evidence to his solipsism,
and does not take account of a narrative hermeneutic of the
self in which continuity and difference coexist through a 'real'
flow of time.[7]

Fortunately there are more promising ways to understand
reconfiguration. T. S. Eliot's appeal to the power of an eternal
or 'timeless' moment did not depend on non-realism. In his
view the poignancy and regrets of the past and the uncertainty
of the future could be dealt with if they are brought into a
present moment of transcendent 'real' time. And because this
is a 'real' transcendent moment, it owns the reality of the past
and future rather than denying it – and that is the basis for
transforming them. Thus the 'moment in the rose garden', the
'footfalls echo in the memory/ Down the passage we did not
take', all that 'might have been and what has been', must be
'remembered . . . involved with past and future' *in time*: 'only
through time time is conquered' ('Burnt Norton'). The experience here involves 'real' time in the sense that the connection

of the present with past and future is not flattened or reduced
to illusion. Instead, they are an essential part of a process.
They belong to a journey or 'exploration' without which their
transformation in the present moment cannot take place. This
is to be the journey of self-giving love:

> . . . something given
> And taken, in a *lifetime's* death, in love,
> Ardour and selflessness and self-surrender. ('Dry Salvages')

> With the drawing of this Love and the voice of this Calling
> We shall not cease from exploration. ('Little Gidding')

Although 'the end of all our exploring/Will be to arrive where
we started', this does not deny the significance of the journey
itself: when we do arrive where we started we shall 'know the
place for the first time' only because of the journey.

The proper name of 'Love' which calls us to this also alerts
us to the reality of God in Eliot's thought and experience. It is
the incarnate Word who gives this transcendent moment
and makes it transforming. This gives further weight to the
need for a 'real' intersection of eternity with time if time is
to be truly reconfigured and healed, and if the self is to be
healed with it. It is arguable whether this follows Platonic–
Augustinian echoes: i.e. whether it is to be taken as a strictly
'timeless' or 'simultaneous' transcendence which breaks into
our present time to transform it.[8] If it is, the 'real' time of our
existence is ultimately relativized after all. But even if read in
this way, the temporal reality of process and exploration in
our experience is still a necessary constituent or backdrop to
this ultimately timeless experience of salvation. It is a very
different picture to the radical postmodern background of
Cupitt's thought. It remains a powerful poetic picture of late-
modern experience. Time must be 'really' reconfigured for the
self to be made whole.

Ricoeur himself, whose general concern with time and selfhood explicitly raised this notion of 'reconfiguring', also looks
to the light of a transcendent eternity. To begin with, the main

hermeneutical tool for understanding ourselves remains the structure of narrative displayed in texts. The overall pattern of a story with its beginning. end and all that lies between helps shape time. It shows the interrelated meaning of events. It demonstrates how the real identity of the self is only fully displayed by reference to purposes and events beyond the present moment of the self. The self's projection of future possibilities becomes part of the intrinsic temporality of the story as of the self, and its potential for being fully itself. But when, crucially, this possibility and 'end' of our story is eternity (rather than death) the basic narrative configuration is given even more meaning. The end of eternity intensifies the meaning of all the temporal events and relations of the story. An eternity which relates all time to itself, even as it transforms it, enhances its significance (*pace* those who assume it is trivialized). Here Ricoeur too is influenced by Augustine, albeit with significant differences. Augustine is more concerned with the narrative extension of time within the human soul than with 'external' stories of textual characters; and, as we have seen, he understands the 'time' of eternity more problematically, as a tenseless simultaneity. Nonetheless, the debt is real and acknowledged.[9]

This appeal to eternity leads naturally to more explicit theological proposals where the specific issue of reconfiguring of time has featured. For instance, the early Barth spoke in much the same language as Eliot and Ricoeur. There is an eternal moment which breaks in to transform *all* time. In Barth's terms this is the Word of Christ which transforms the self and gives us our real identity in Christ. This again makes clear the connection between redeemed time and redeemed self.[10] The ontological possibility for this, as we have seen, is established by a doctrine of God's being which includes a 'perfected' or 'authentic' form of temporality within his own eternity. This provides the potential for God to enter our time and redeem it. It offers both the necessary connection and the necessary otherness for an effective act of redemption.

Other major theological treatments take their orientation more particularly from eschatology. Moltmann wants to construe redemption as 'a movement which runs from the future to the past, not from the past to the future'.[11] The eschatological event gathers up the past to ensure that nothing need be lost or unredeemed. It ensures that the forward march of time leaves behind no irrevocable victims in its wake. This is a transcendental event of the world's future which can be associated with the biblical 'Last Day' or Day of Judgement. It is not clear how this works conceptually in relation to what we know of historical reality with its inexorable march forward. It seems to function symbolically to describe how *meaning* can flow from future events to transform past events once we have reached that future (i.e. there is no literal reverse flow of time to make this happen). But not all is left to the future in this way. The time of the present is also transformed by its orientation *into* the future which awaits it. Expressing the transcendent meaning as 'ahead' of us like this allows the present is to be changed 'now' because it is already part of a larger narrative heading forwards. This underwrites the commitment to act within the world to change it (and ourselves), rather than be passively bound to the present or world-denying.[12] In this way the significance of acting in the present is secured – though the final cause of this motivation is still the meaning that the future gives back to the past and present. Such meaning comes explicitly in the form of the promise of a God who is faithful and able to do all this. Moltmann makes clear the theological connections between this sort of integration of time and the integration of human identity (usually considered generically rather than individually). The history and full identity of human life is established just because it is part of God's whole 'eternal' history in his own trinitarian life. God expresses his own relational and 'historical' identity through the history of the world, and thereby brings humanity its proper identity in himself.[13]

Pannenberg also has an eschatological orientation. Events do not have their completion until their full meaning is received, and that comes from the future as much as the past or present. Further events can transform the meaning of present events. In the huge horizon of the end of all things, that transformation is definitive. The archetype of this process is the resurrection of Jesus Christ, which acts retrospectively to transform the meaning of his life and death.[14] It is, again, a way of reading time backwards in the meaning it bestows, and indeed the 'being' it bestows.[15] For Pannenberg this is even more explicitly linked to the being and becoming of human identity.[16] As with Jesus Christ, who we are only emerges through this process of time in which the 'we' in the present must interact with God's wider purposes in society and the world, and above all with the completion of them in the future. It is the call of this future which provides the sense of vocation, particularized with each person, though not necessarily confined to a single vocation. We find our identity through our vocation(s). We are not entirely determined by this call: the essential mystery of this future still leaves open some sense of provisionality, contingency, and creativity. This means that the eschatological event of Jesus Christ does not entirely foreclose on the mystery, as some critics have complained. [17] Nonetheless, it does give some real shape to it. The future is already life-giving to the present.

Another kind of reconfiguration of time has been offered by David Ford in his meditations on the self.[18] He owes much to his engagement with Ricoeur, and there are clear similarities at some points. He takes seriously the temporal view of a narrative self where the past persists in the present, at least as an analogical kind of repetition – well described, therefore, as 're[con]figuring'. *Where* this happens, however, is best displayed for Ford in what he calls 'Eucharistic' time. This sort of event (i.e. the Eucharist) repeats non-identically pivotal events of the past in a way which 'pays a debt' to the past but also appropriates it for future possibilities: 'in gratitude the past is repeated in such a way that it is fruitful in a new way for the present and future'. As with Pannenberg, this is not meant to foreclose the future by reading off from the events recalled a strict paradigm for the future. It is a creative engagement with the past and with the dynamism of it, rather than a privileged access to some window on a completed metanarrative. This creativity is expressed through the experience of praise evoked in the event of eucharistic worship and remembrance, which (like music) operates by a non-identical repetition, opening up what Ford calls 'endless improvisation' on the basic themes, the logic of Kierkegaard's view that 'repetition is always a transcendence'.[19] The Gospel of John's 'innovative re-telling' of the eucharistic events, with its ethical imperative to move out from them in the Spirit to love, is another example of this creative process of refiguring time. And this is all affirmed explicitly as the 'habitus' in which the self is formed: it is 'an apprenticeship which helps the self to flourish'.[20]

There are questions to be asked of Ford. It is not clear to what extent the liturgical event of eucharist is being taken illustratively or constitutively. How can such transformation of time be experienced outside that particular 'habitus' or tradition? This is a pressing question when, as indicated before, so few now live within it. Even more crucially, his main concern is with the flow of good past events into present and future – but how does this deal with the bad? There are also questions to be put to the other theological proposals. The vulnerabilities of Barth's positivism of revelation and its underlying ontology have already been mentioned. Moltmann's and Pannenberg's confidence about the future has also received ample critique in a climate where there is so much suspicion of 'completeness' or 'closure'.[21]

But these criticisms do not touch the main point, which has been simply to demonstrate the extent to which the problems of self and the problems of time are integrally related. They are related in some of the most telling literature, philosophy and theology of this late-modern period. By the same token, the healing of self and our broken experience of time is also shown as inseparable. The common appeal to 'eternity', whether of transcendent timelessness, transcendent timefulness, or the sheer totality of the present moment, expresses in radically different ways this common quest: to integrate time not just conceptually *but to establish where and who we are*. The specific appeal to God reinforces this. Whenever God is invoked, implicitly by poets or explicitly by theologians, this fundamental relationship between fulfilled personal identity and redeemed or reconfigured temporality is displayed.

Self, time and faithfulness

All this offers further warrant for the significance of faithfulness. If the integration of our experience of time is critical, then we have to find ways to inhabit as much time as possible. The kind of relationship we need with all this time is a dynamic, redeeming relationship. In some way or other we have to move backwards and forwards through time. We must do this to allow the widest possible scope of meaning from the past and (where possible) the future to inform the 'eternity' of the present. By definition this will require us constantly to draw on resources of meaning and purpose outside our own immediate sense of self. We have to relate to the meaning of people and events on a wider spectrum of time than our immediate experience of it normally includes. The healing of time and our own identity therefore entails paying all possible attention to the meaning of other people and events through time. Conversely, and perhaps better: paying all possible attention to the meaning of other people and events through time entails our healing in time. Either way this is precisely the meaning of faithfulness. It is the motivation to stay with people through time and change. It is a dynamic, redeeming, engagement with people and events through all possible time.

The natural means by which we have access to both past and future sharpens this need for faithfulness. The past has to be engaged through the individual memory, and beyond that through the corporate repositories of tradition and collective memory. This requires us to have been there ourselves, inhabiting those memories. We do this either by personal involvement in past events and relationships, or by belonging to a community which corporately bears a narrative tradition and a wider collective memory. Either way, it requires some staying power, some faithfulness. Likewise with the future. Access to future meaning can only be gained by individual anticipation or prediction, and beyond that through the corporate projection of a narrative tradition which looks forwards as well as backwards (a scientific or religious meta-narrative). Again, this requires our persistent presence. The meaning we draw back from the future in this way can only have its full effect if we go on to inhabit that future, faithfully, within that broad framework of meaning: i.e. staying with the narrative tradition to which we have belonged in the past. It does not mean being uncritical. But it does require faithfulness.

There are difficulties, of course. In relation to the past memory and tradition are selective, and they are invariably 'prejudices'. There is no objective history recoverable to integrate with our present experience. But as Gadamer has shown, the Enlightenment 'prejudice against prejudices' needs to be exposed.[22] The whole point of trawling the past is not to recover an illusory fixed meaning and then try to change it or come to terms with it, but to see that its full meaning never was fixed but open to its future. That is how and why our current perception of it can be a redeeming one. It underlines again the value of a continuous and faithful subject who straddles past and present, *being there* to help make the redeeming connections. In relation to the future there are even greater limits, and a different kind of contingency. The meaning which it projects back to all that precedes it does not just depend on its effective anticipation and appropriation in the present. It depends on something like that future actually being created by those involved in the story. This naturally cannot be guaranteed. No individual or community can wholly determine the future. But again it underlines the value of a faithful commitment to stay with the story, to help determine that future as far as possible.

As we have seen, a theological perspective adds a further critical dimension to this. The doctrine of a transcendent God who is faithful to us through all time and eternity creates new ontological and moral possibilities for our own faithfulness. In Pannenberg's terms, a transcendent God has some power over the future. Out of that he is able to give us now some assured shape to our future. The Christ event has brought that shape into our historical horizons of meaning. It is not all left to guesswork. It draws us in a determinate direction, even though the contingencies still have to be worked out in time. Our belonging to the Christian tradition is our participation in this given metanarrative of the future. In the same way the transcendence of God involves full access to the past. In Moltmann's terms it entails the capacity to set all wrongs right in the full light of the 'eternal' eschatological event. This is the basis for us to participate in the same process, however limited our access or capabilities. It underwrites the meaning of it. It is much the same point that I have argued elsewhere: God's universal scope of activity (in space, time and eternity) is both conceptually and theologically compelling just because it provides the necessary conditions for full divine redemption. Specifically, it undergirds a moral notion of forgiveness, rather than mere forgetfulness or retribution.[23] Recast in the terms of this discussion, these are all aspects of divine faithfulness to his creation – which gives an ultimate basis for our limited attempts to inhabit time in a faithful way.

A theological perspective also reminds us about the value of particularity within the temporal flow. The drive to inhabit the whole flow of time does not imply a uniform meaning to all time. While the whole story and all its unfolding relationships have meaning, there are always pivotal moments within the narrative which uniquely focus or constitute that wider reach of meaning. Eliot's quartets spiral constantly round such moments. David Ford reminds us of them in his treatment of eucharistic time and cites other examples in ordinary 'non-religious' human experience.[24] The christological heart of the Christian metanarrative is the critical reminder of it in wider theology.

To be sure, even the wider theological perspective does not deliver to us all that belongs to God. The limits of our finitude mean we will not experience *full* access to past and future. We always have to pass to the future with some of the past unresolved. Nonetheless, the greater the commitment to connecting as much as we can through time, the more meaning is recovered and the more creative the relationships become.

The unresolved will be more bearable when it is held within a generally full and faithful commitment. When the present is as 'eternal' as possible the identity of the self can incorporate the unresolved without disintegrating. By contrast, a temptation to cut and run, the attempt to begin a new and unconnected story every time there is something unresolved, has quite a different effect. It emasculates that present moment. The self withers. Implications in specific areas of ordinary human living, such as marriage, kinship loyalties, working practices, will be looked at later. For now, it is simply the critical nature of this broad principle of faithfulness which needs registering. Kundera was right. Without faithfulness we splinter into a thousand fragments. Time and self alike stand or fall apart on the basis of faithfulness. They have both become particularly problematic in our current context of rapid change – and faithfulness presents itself as the key weapon with which to fight the spiritual battles which have ensued.

7

LIMITS AND POSSIBILITIES

Resources for faithfulness: God, community, change

If ought implies can, then the call to faithfulness must have some basis in the structures of our existence to make it possible. The framework of these structures has been laid out. A metanarrative which incorporates meaning from the future and the past provides the theoretical basis. Within the Christian metanarrative, specific doctrines of God, his love, faithfulness, sovereignty, omnipresence and eschatology provide the ontological basis and moral motivation to respond. The summons of a God who is himself faithful and able to undergird all our action is therefore the most profound resource and reason for human faithfulness. When this call is embodied in a tradition-bearing community with a supporting context of discourse and social practice, faithfulness becomes all the more possible in practice.

The basic structure of human personal identity which makes faithfulness possible has also been laid out. We are essentially temporal but unitary selves, defined by our relations in community and susceptible to change, but enduring as single subjects through the varied narrative of our lives. We are not wholly determined, but have some limited capacities for free response and action. We act largely out of a character formed by our response within our social relations and the events of this narrative. This is the outline of the anthropological resources for human faithfulness. It is part of the Christian tradition, but resonates in other anthropologies as well.

So if we ask how we can have the will (or disposition) to be

faithful, the answer is clear enough. The sustained will to be
faithful is best formed within a relationship to God embodied
in a character-forming community and set of social practices.
This relationship with God may or may not be explicitly realized in those practices: nonetheless, the specific value of a
confessing and worshipping community, forming the character of a worshipping self, certainly needs to be recognized.[1]
Any sort of answer like this still has to live with difficult questions about the freedom of that will. The nature of causation at
the nexus of individual, social and divine agency is opaque,
and the extent of individual responsibility within that nexus is
hard to fathom. Grace, determinism and freewill, individual
and corporate responsibility, qualify each other without ever
quite explaining how. Their relationship has always resisted
easy analysis, and not just within Christian theology. But there
is no need here to resolve that. What matters is simply to
register that some sort of *sustained* will or disposition is
required, and it is most likely to be found and formed precisely
within a narrative tradition and social support of this kind.

As indicated, the role of community support in sustaining faithfulness is evident in any general social practices
which provide public recognition for personal commitments,
whether or not it is part of an explicit religious tradition (the
institution of marriage is an obvious example). However,
when a religious tradition is made explicit, its full resources
can be more easily brought to bear. And within the Christian
tradition these are very evident. The weakness of the will is
consistently forgiven, remade, remotivated within the continuing narrative of God's grace and the practices of the community which convey that grace. The narrative of Peter provides
a seminal example of this. Peter is picked up, dusted down
and set on his way again in the path of his discipleship not
once but many times over. A pivotal moment of this process
is the lakeside encounter with the risen Christ where his
threefold denial of faithfulness is matched with a process of
threefold probing and recommissioning. In this way the
meaning of discipleship is held within a narrative of
continuing, responsive, divine love and faithfulness. Liturgical

practices of the Church continue that narrative in various ways, in confession and absolution, baptism and confirmation, communion and covenant services. Its substantive social life and practices should do the same. Internally this means the Church should be using these resources to constantly renew and recommission the roles of its members within its own life, to help sustain them in their faithfulness. Externally, it should be employing its resources to renew its backing for all social goals which provide a similar support. Marriage is one example, and there are others, to be considered further in the following chapters. All such social support and continuous formation of character will help sustain faithful living through situations of tragedy, perplexity and moral conflict, as well as straightforward sin and failure.[2]

Another key factor in sustaining the faithful disposition is the self's own capacity to incorporate change, without ceasing to be itself. As we have seen, it is a feature of personal identity to be able to be fulfilled through change rather than threatened by it. This arises out of the essential connectedness and temporality both of ourselves and the relations and traditions which form us. It also refers us back to the disparate elements of contingency and givenness which constitute our identity. Some aspects of our identity are self-chosen, not imposed by others or by circumstance. This is the clear correlate of having some measure of personal meaning and freedom. Equally, a good deal of our identity is given to us from beyond ourselves, and needs to be if we are not to be entirely self-centred, solipsistic selves. We saw this to be intrinsic to Christian anthropology, as well as more widely accepted. The particular point here is that even when these 'outside' determinants of our identity change beyond our control, faithfulness to them is still possible because of these other capacities of response within ourselves. This is no threat to ourselves precisely because our identity is sufficiently complex to accommodate change without ceasing to be itself. There is always a unitary, enduring person to whom these changes occur, and whose integrity is not necessarily threatened, but sometimes enhanced, even by radical change.

Much the same point is made by Margaret Farley in her discussion of commitment in interpersonal relationships.[3] Her analysis deals mostly with motivation and authenticity in personal commitments. For this she draws on Marcel's existential concerns to help her. A full personal commitment of fidelity is more than mere 'constancy', because it involves our own personal being or 'presence' in the relationship, not just the performance of a legal duty. To retain that personal presence in the relationship therefore requires the accommodation of change. To be truly ourselves we must be able to incorporate change in ourselves as well as in the relationship in a creative way. This in turn requires embracing our own past and future in a particular dynamic way – another reminder of the importance for our identity of inhabiting the whole of time, not just the present moment. Thus: 'if we are not to be "unhitched" from our commitments the secret is to hold together our past and future, but to do so in a way that does not leave us with something static and unchanging'. In this '"way of fidelity", therefore, we change yet we endure; our relationship changes, yet it endures'.[4]

Vincent Brummer takes a similar position in his analysis of love. He refutes the view that change in another necessarily means an end to commitment and the inevitability of a sequence of relationships, each one replacing the other.[5]

If lovers respond to changing circumstances in ways which are incompatible, they will grow apart. If however they seek to respond in ways which are compatible, their personal identities will change and develop in concert and they will grow together in the course of time.[6]

There are qualifications to this. This sort of love depends on mutual motivation to respond to each other's changes. In Brummer's view it cannot be sustained unilaterally. Likewise I would add that our capacity to change can be limited by some experiences: circumstances can result in the sort of depression and hurt in an individual, or demoralization in an institution, which paralyses at the very point where change needs to be exercised. I shall return to this later. Nonetheless, the positive point remains. The capacity to change responsively is a vital resource for the fulfilment of faithful relationship. This is worked out by Brummer in terms of interpersonal love, but it holds true for sustaining faithfulness in other contexts. For example, commitment from and to institutions or traditions is subject to similar dynamics. They too are essentially temporal, dynamic realities, so there is no reason why they too cannot change without destroying their identity. This means that 'creative fidelity' must be possible in the same way in institutions as it is between individuals.

Limits of faithfulness: the nature of commitment

Such are some of the resources for faithfulness. But what, if any, are its limits? Theology is not an easy starting place here. For God there are no obvious limits. He remains faithful, even when he judges. Hell can be invoked as a sign of limits, but only in some forms of the doctrine. So perhaps it is the fragility, finitude and rebellion of human being which really lies behind the question of limits, not God's being. But even here there is no straightforward theological answer. In the varying circumstances of the human condition, how do we know what constitutes a *legitimate* limit to our faithfulness?

One way of assessing this is to step back for a moment from the theological blueprint and simply attend to common practice. How do we normally understand and justify the commitments we make and break? It is especially worth looking at the commitments which inaugurate faithful relationships. Some commitments deliberately build in limitations from the beginning. But there are also contextual factors which commonly affect the nature of commitment already in being. Either way, do common practices and common meanings shed light on our limits?

Farley offers this summary of the factors which appear to limit a commitment or provide legitimate release.[7] An obligation may not hold if (1) there is no real commitment in the first place; (2) the other releases me; (3) it becomes impossible to

fulfil; (4) there are competing obligations. The first two factors
are largely self-explanatory. In the last two factors she offers
this further explanation. 'Impossibility' is carefully defined. It
may not be enough simply to cite lack of moral or emotional
resources as a reason for finding a commitment impossible,
nor is it enough simply to cite personal change. Social, cultural
and economic factors, are also likely to be relevant. In marriage, for example, the level of social and economic availability
of divorce, and the extent of social support for marriage,
will significantly affect the threshold at which a particular
marriage commitment will appear 'impossible'. Moreover, in
most moral discourse there must also be some factor which
makes it impossible to fulfil the good *of the other*, if the release
is to be justified. In that sense, the commitment must still be
fulfilled in a more general sense (the good of the other), even
though it has become impossible in its more specific original
sense. A similar explanation is offered in situations where
there are competing obligations. These only justify release
from an existing commitment when it can be seen as instrumental to some larger commitment which remains fulfilled.
For example, it may be justified to lay down a commitment to
work for some specific charity in order to serve some wider
social cause.

Analysing commitments in this way acknowledges some
limits imposed by social context: but even these are only legitimate if residual commitment can be retained in some way.
The overriding concern is still to serve what Farley calls a 'just'
love even when particular commitments have to be curtailed.
The goal remains to fulfil some aspects of an original commitment in order to be true or just to the relationship which is
ending. In this way we are never released from the fundamental commitment to love the other, whatever limits there are to
the specific focus of that commitment. There is an echo here of
Royce's insistence of loyalty as an ultimate principle which
can never be totally abandoned or negotiated away – though
Farley herself roots this concern in Christian faith rather than
philosophical idealism. She refers explicitly to the essentially
faithful God who always gives *himself* in covenant relation-

ship, and who cannot withdraw or deny himself in them, however much the specific expression of faithfulness may have to change (another echo of Marcel).

It is an illuminating analysis. Nonetheless, the discussion of limits needs to be taken further. In particular, more needs to be said about the objective structures of relationship such as 'responsibility' and 'role', which Farley's more existential analysis does not deal with so much. This is important. When the notion of faithfulness is defined through responsibility and role, some of its limits in principle emerge more clearly. It also provides a better basis for a theological perspective about this.

Responsibility and role

The notions of responsibility and faithfulness overlap. Any adequate concept of responsibility is bound to entail the same sort of social and temporal understanding of personal identity which underlies a call to faithfulness. Thus a mature analysis of responsibility, according to William Schweiker,

> designates something about the temporal character of the self. We understand ourselves, we have our moral identities, as historical agents in relation to others and the world. Persons exists as selves in a moral space of relations through time . . . Responsibility has a retrospective and future orientated character to it . . . Being responsible entails a commitment to self-constancy through time . . . Without the persistence of identity through time, without some conception of the 'self' bound to memory, hope and capacities for self-reflection, the idea of responsibility becomes vacuous.[8]

Schweiker sees this responsible self formed within social practices and relations of a community which is itself formed through time by a tradition where there is a dynamic continuity between past, present and future.

This represents an integration of a number of strands or theories of responsibility, drawn from various historical, philosophical and theological sources. It includes a Kantian focus on the individual good will responsible for acting out a consistent moral imperative of practical reason. But it goes beyond this. It takes account of the moral imperative written into our essential being which Tillich provides by grounding our being in the Being of God. This too is only part of Schweiker's picture, because our actual being does not fully express this essential being. Full responsibility lies neither in acting out of the 'abstraction' of a rational good will, nor in appealing to straightforward human instincts of human nature, but in the integration of our actual and essential or 'true' being. This has to happen in relation to other persons, overcoming our estrangement from ourselves and others through love. Even this is not the whole view because it does not take sufficient account of the other historical and social goods and goals of life. To integrate the self, even in relation to others, still does not secure the self in a wider sense of responsibility for fulfilling social roles and communal enterprises.

Here F. H. Bradley and ultimately Aristotle are needed to provide the further dimension. They offer the groundwork for a social theory of responsibility in which the main concern is not the discrete actions of an individual agent, but the fulfilment of social roles by persons bound in the social practices of a community. The moral focus of human identity then becomes the character of people formed within and fitting such social practices and roles carried out over time – and particular actions are only considered secondarily in so far as they flow from that character and its social formation. As we have seen, Hauerwas is the one who radically appropriates this in theological terms.

Yet this too needs modification. The danger is that it might reduce the meaning of responsibility wholly to the performance of a social role within community beyond criticism. So it also needs some sense of a free responsive self in dialogue with others, not just assimilated to them – both 'The Other' (Barth) and others (H. R. Niebuhr).

Such are the contours of Schweiker's 'integrated' theory of responsibility.[9] It is neither individualistic, nor socially oppressive, neither deontological nor wholly utilitarian. It coheres well with the responsible and faithful self of Christian theology, which finds its moral identity not simply in the evaluation of particular actions, nor simply by membership of a religious community, but in the richer, responsive state or relation of being in Christ and being a follower of Christ. Its emphasis on the social and temporal dimensions of moral responsibility mirrors the more general argument of this book. It belongs to a moral definition of identity which then requires fulfilment by faithfulness.

The main point to highlight, however, has to do with any *limits* to responsibility entailed by all this – which, in turn, will qualify the meaning of faithfulness. And the critical notion here is the way 'role' has emerged as a central feature of responsibility. It seems that roles give us our major sphere of responsibility. *Yet some roles clearly come to an end, and our responsibility with them.* Moreover, this is sometimes beyond our control. Roles, after all, are part of a social context which depends on the will and circumstances of others, which can change. They are given by others as much as self-chosen. This adds a particular dimension to the meaning of 'impossibility' when we are trying to sustain faithful relationship. It is some-times *causally* impossible to exercise a role of commitment unilaterally if role circumstances have changed. For example, in relationships of personal love a commitment *cannot* be responsibly maintained if the other decides to enter into another publicly committed and exclusive relationship (like marriage). It is the same in other kinds of relationships. In employment neither employer or employee can continue in their role without some form of consent from the other. Even where mutual consent is maintained there is an obvious sense in which death or retirement will eventually end the role and much of the responsibility which goes with it.

So does this mean that faithfulness – a commitment through time and change – simply cannot be sustained whenever there is a limited role involved? The question presses hard just because socially defined roles are such vital ingredients within our identity. We are given a role as children of our parents, members of our birth community and country; we may choose a role to be partners in marriage or parents of children; we may inherit, or feel called into, a role as farmer, teacher, soldier, civil servant. In all these cases the origin of role varies, but at the same time their significance is undisputed: *role helps constitute selfhood*. That is why faithfulness cannot sidestep role if it is to maintain its claim to fulfil identity. Yet roles seem to set clear limits which seriously compromise the imperative. How then can faithfulness operate with limited roles?

The answer has to be a qualified one. On the one hand this challenge which 'role' puts to responsibility and faithfulness is not wholesale. This is because social roles, though important, are not the whole of our identity. This was clear in the anthropological definitions of identity offered before. It was also apparent in Schweiker's integrated definition of responsibility. There is a transcendence and freedom in both God and ourselves over against any particular social or ecclesiastical context. It means we are not entirely reduced to our social roles. This must mean that we may have some way of expressing responsibility and faithfulness beyond particular roles, even when they come to end. It returns us to Farley's concerns – and some of her solutions. Faithfulness may still be able to express some sort of 'just love' even when it is no longer possible to fulfil a particular role. Faithfulness can still press us to look to the well-being of the other, even if a particular kind of role within the relationship has to come to an end. Because there is more to our identity than our roles, this may always be a possibility. Ought *does* imply can, at least to some extent. On the other hand the significance of changing roles clearly qualifies the 'can' in some respects. There is a constraint when roles define and limit responsibility in determinate ways – and this will affect the *way* in which faithfulness can be exercised, even though its meaning may also transcend particular roles.

In short, the notion of faithfulness cannot ignore the question of role, and the question has to be pressed further. Roles certainly matter in social practice, but how much should they matter? Above all, is there any theological perspective on this?

Roles and a theological basis

A theological basis for evaluating role has been found by some in basic trinitarian doctrines of God. The divine–human analogy which flows from these doctrines is explicitly used in this way. The suggestion is to read off a normative understanding of role from the relationship of the three persons of God in trinitarian theology.

At one level this is highly problematic. On the one hand role seems vital and enduring to the divine identity. A perichoretic view of trinitiarian relations means that each 'person' constitutes the other's eternal identity by virtue of the particular role played. Thus the Father is only the Father because he is Father of the Son, and vice versa. The Spirit then constitutes that Father–Son relationship by virtue of its own role between them or in relation to both (depending on the nuances of the Augustinian–Greek spectrum of trinitarianism). On the other hand these roles can be presented less decisively. Although they might seem well-defined within the immanent Trinity, they are exercised jointly and flexibly in God's activity in the world. In creation and redemption Father, Son and Spirit are all active in interchangeable ways. These roles seem to have elements of fluidity and contingency. At the point of incarnation the Son laid down his equality with the Father and assumed radical dependency and subordination, only to change back at his glorified 'return' to eternity. So while Sonship (generally) may be essential to the eternal identity of God, its specific meaning seems changeable, at least when projected into the conditions of space, time, fallenness. This can then be read back into the essential Trinity. Encouraged by feminist and postmodern concern about the oppression of any fixed hierarchy, it suggests a more dynamic doctrine of perichoresis. Within this all roles are essentially interchangeable in the 'dance' of the Trinity. There are relations of Fatherhood (or parenthood), Sonship (or childhood) and Spirit within the Trinity, but no role that is fixed or particular to any one person. An even more radical deconstruction dissolves the residual substance ontology of persons altogether.

There are only shifting relations, no particular 'persons' at all.[10]

This last move highlights the underlying difficulty of the whole analogy, at any stage of its construal. The meaning of the divine persons is not equivalent to human persons (except in the most tri-theistic of social doctrines of trinity). Reducing them to mere shifting relations either signals the final bankruptcy of the analogy, or else it reinstates the analogy by reducing human personhood itelf to mere relations. Either way this fails to do justice to the theology and anthropology of the full Christian narrative. One way or another, therefore, the notion of divine role is problematic as a modelling for human role.

Yet it could still offer some general parameters. First, there is the notion that *some* particular roles belong to divine identity, however fluid and qualified. While the particular meaning of role within the incarnate life of God may be contingent, role per se is still the expression of God being himself. As such role is not mere playfulness, just a mask put on to entertain an audience in some lesser theatre of reality. This is important to establish. Both Aristotelian and Platonic notions of 'person' tended to view role as an indication of this sort of insubstantiality. By contrast, the impetus to conceive the notion of 'person' as more than a passing 'mask' was derived precisely from the pressures of Christian trinitarian theology.[11] Secondly, however, there is this notion that role is not wholly fixed but can fulfil the divine identity when it is jointly and contingently expressed. This too will be valuable. Taken together they provide parameters which permit some useful distinctions.

They suggest first that there can be a fundamental difference between roles. They vary in significance. This confirms common sense. In ordinary human living there are roles of pure playfulness. We literally put on masks sometimes, in a theatre. Metaphorically we frequently cast ourselves and others in different roles to play games, in common discourse and in all human relationships. These are voluntary, transient assumptions of a changed aspect of our identity, undertaken for a variety of reasons. They can be manipulative or merry: aspects of engineering situations to our end, or sheer enjoyment. But either way they occur at a superficial level which does not belong to our essential identity. To be sure, something like acting a part in a play or playing the tourist may matter to us, simply because being playful in general may be an important part of our identity. But there is still no need to be too solemn about these particular roles. We can take them up and lay them down without needing to raise fundamental questions of faithfulness. It need not compromise our identity if we do not play that particular part or visit that country again.

Equally, there clearly are roles which do matter, at a different level. There are roles which help to constitute our essential identity – and in these roles faithfulness will matter profoundly. Trinitarian doctrine in itself will not help us read off which particular roles carry this weight. For this we shall need the biblical narratives and the wider tradition of Christian theology, working through empirical experience (as we have seen, these at least offer some presumptions about marriage, kinship, community, nation, religion). Nonetheless, trinitarian theology does give some ultimate *warrant* for what emerges in this way. It gives weight to the general perception that some roles are essential, even though they may vary in nature and significance. That is an important distinction to be maintained in this world of constant change and fluid, flickering relations. There is play – but not all is play.

Trinitarian theology can also teach the difference between fixed and fluid notions of role. It suggests that even significant roles need not be static. As we have seen, the general parameters of trinitarianism permit, even require, a measure of fluidity in role: roles need not be exclusive and may be exercised jointly. So the meaning of some may change radically as identity is expressed in different contexts. This means that faithfulness in role cannot be legislated as an absolute, prescriptive dogma. It must be seen as a disposition which can (faithfully) accommodate this sort of fluidity and change. It confirms the importance of character and disposition more than rule and regulation.

To translate this into specific terms for human living will again need more than trinitarian theology. It must draw on wider resources and those presumptions already set by biblical narratives and wider historical experience. And these readily support the general point. For example, the loyalty appropriate within a particular religious tradition or community clearly requires change. It does not mean a static allegiance. It may permit, even require, radical changes in that tradition. That is the origin of all painful reformation required by prophets within both Judaism and Christianity, and the even more painful conversion from one to the other. The Pauline theology of Romans 9–11, already noted, is a case in point: the grafting together of Christian and Jew will require the role of the faithful Jew to be significantly *changed* in the process, even though there is no ultimate severing of allegiance. Similarly, the role of a faithful partner in marriage may have to face the possibility of change. The change may be radical. A kind of ending may even occur. Breakdown of marriage and bereavement both feature in biblical and Christian tradition, as well as ordinary experience. When this happens, I shall be arguing later that it still shows this pattern: the faithful facing of these experiences entails the radical reconstruction of a role, rather than the fixed reimposition of a role (or a complete end to it).

Faithfulness is also exercised in this way where there is conflict of roles. Here again the biblical narrative displays the resources of a disposition which can reshape a role, rather than a set of fixed rules which simply reasserts one role at the expense of another. For example, there is conflict between Abraham's role as father to Isaac and obedient servant to Yahweh, or between Jesus' role as son to his earthly parents and his divine sonship. Kierkegaard's reflections impose a grid of polar opposites, an 'either-or', on this sort of situation. But mature reflection on the narratives suggests that roles are radically reshaped in the faithful process of conflict, not simply jettisoned or reimposed. Abraham's identity in relation to both his son and his God is certainly redefined, and Jesus' identity is more deeply revealed – but no role is wholly cast aside. Thus Isaac remains Abraham's son to pass on the lineage of Israel, and Mary remains Jesus' concern even at his death. This too is an important notion to maintain about role. All is not play, but there is still something to play with.

More detailed discussion of these issues follows in the next chapter. For now it is just a basic principle which is being supplied from this sort of theological background. Social roles (apart from the merely playful) are vital constituents of identity, in which faithfulness matters supremely. But they can also be a flexible, changing, dynamic notion. This means that the faithful exercise of a role may not be best determined by fixed rules, but arises better out of a *disposition* of faithfulness. This clearly mirrors the general meaning of faithfulness already established: i.e. it is an aspect of character and disposition rather than a specific ethical injunction.

Wider views of role

This is not simply a theological construction of role and its significance. Alasdair MacIntyre's historical and philosophical analysis of the significance of social role in different epochs offers a similar picture. It confirms its importance specifically for identity, and particularly when it is arises out of character formed out of a community with its own narrative character and tradition. At best this integrates a person within himself and with her world, so that there is little conflict or fragmentation between the two. In this way

> the individual is identified and constituted in and through certain of his or her roles, those roles which bind the individual to the communities in and through which alone specifically human goods are attained. I confront the world as a member of this family, that household, this clan, this tribe, this city, this nation, this kingdom. There is no 'I' apart from these.[12]

For MacIntyre this integrated state of affairs was found in the ancient and medieval worlds – and in the novels of Jane

Austen. However, it is conspicuously absent from the late-postmodern world where the 'I' has been cast adrift from the security of these roles by plural and fragmented narratives. In this contemporary world the self can only adopt the disconnected roles which such a society can offer (such as managerialism, therapy, pleasure-seeking).

As a portrait of specific cultures of past and present MacIntyre's picture uses a broad brush. But as an articulation of the nature and potentialities of social role it is acute – and confirms much of the theological analysis. What it further reminds us is that the limits to role are not just set by mutual consent of individuals and corporatebodies, nor just by circumstantial change, or death, but by much wider changes in social context. For if MacIntyre has illustrated nothing else in his project, he has certainly demonstrated the difficulty of re-forming a society of integrated roles, identity, narrative, once it has disintegrated. Here too the possibilities for faithfulness will be directly affected. When the only available roles no longer nourish a satisfying identity, a key context for learning faithfulness disappears. This is the vicious circle (for example) that a marginalized youth faces so acutely if he comes from a broken home, disintegrated local 'community', no religion, and short-term employment. In the face of this, a strong theological basis to faithfulness will not give up its call to fulfilment through faithfulness. It will want to exploit the flexibilities in the meaning of role as best it can, rather than abandon all sense of role. It will want to redeem some kind of faithfulness within whatever scraps of worthwhile belonging and activity are remaindered. It will want to do this as part of all wider attempts to reform society as a whole. But it will not pretend that it is easy.

Such are some of the possibilities and constraints for faithfulness . As with any virtue it has to be exercised and learned both individually and corporately. It has to happen in a theological context of sin freedom, fallenness. Above all, it has to happen in dynamic and fast-changing social contexts – which are not always conducive to it.

False faithfulness

Finally, faithfulness has to be exercised and earned alongside its own parodies. For there is such a thing as false faithfulness. It becomes false, for example, when it is a tool of oppression by the powerful and collusion by the victim. It becomes false if it is used to fossilize a relationship in a status quo which is stultifying, damaging, unjust. The dangers arise partly out of its natural setting in a metanarrative. It is a commonplace criticism of postmodernity that metanarratives are ready vehicles of what is called premature 'closure'. That is, they 'fix' an overall closed context of meaning, usually to serve the interests of those who create or police the structure. This is liable to be imposed oppressively on others, leaving no room to open up new horizons of meaning. It also arises out of the particular nature of faithfulness as a timeful disposition of commitment, which is obviously susceptible to stagnation. In these ways the call to faithfulness within a metanarrative easily becomes just a tool for cementing allegiance within a closed system.[13]

The possibility of this sort of imprisonment is evident throughout biblical, traditional and modern worlds of experience alike. It is a story told in the complex New Testament treatment of both 'law' and 'temple'. Faithfulness to these had become false. Some liberation was required from fixed notions of law and temple which had been defining the Jewish peoples' identity in an enclosed way. A distinct but parallel process of liberation was required in the Reformation period. Christian identity had become too enclosed in the practices of the medieval Church, which were self-justifying rather than open to divine grace.[14] More generally, the marriage of Aristotelian metaphysics and Christian metanarrative had produced another kind of imprisonment. It was a superstructure which enclosed reason. Scientific method had to struggle hard to emerge. The Enlightenment then created its own forms of oppression leading to the liberation of some aspects of postmodernism. In individual and personal life there have always been specific experiences of imprisonment within social role and status, within family life in general, and within marriage in particular. In all these contexts, notions of loyalty and faithfulness have been exploited to bolster the prison doors, rather than unlock them.

This is obviously a false notion of faithfulness. It is a travesty of its true meaning seen in its proper theological setting. This true faithfulness is a disposition of character, not a fixed law. It incorporates change in the fulfilment of personal identity and in relation to roles which are not necessarily fixed. Its power to maintain integrity in the face of conflicting loyalties or forced closure lies in its attempt at creative continuities, not simply dogmatic repetition. Above all, it is placed within a narrative tradition which is predicated on new meaning flowing from the future into the past and present, so that its claim to inhabit all time is not a restrictive claim. These are clear reasons why a true Christian notion of faithfulness is not vulnerable to deconstruction in principle – though of course it can easily err in practice, so vigilance is always necessary.

Another kind of danger to be noted is quite different. The false faithfulness bound up with the psychology of victims is not always a collusion with an oppressive structure. It may simply be a failure of nerve. The appeal to faithfulness may simply be made to clothe cowardice with a moral lining. In other words, we sometimes fail to break out of structures of living with institutions or people simply because we cannot face the emotional cost.

Admittedly this is very difficult to judge. The difficulty of it is a pervasive theme of literature where deeper ambivalences of motive, psychological profile and outcome can be explored at leisure through an extended narrative. Thomas Hardy is a fine exponent of this. *The Return of the Native* is a good example. Characters who attempt to break out of oppressive old loyalties are granted a 'reality' and significance in the plot which is denied to others, but they precipitate a tragic outcome (which is the cost of this sort of courage). Characters with less emotional energy to take action and face its cost survive on their own terms. In one sense they remain more intact. There is, therefore, no clear moral evaluation of the individuals at the heart of this. It is unprofitable to judge character and motive when it is so constrained by psychological type and the wider buffeting of surrounding social forces and circumstances. As in literature so in life. 'Failure of nerve' is not uncommon, but it should not be too quickly judged. Particular individuals are operating within a complex of psychological and social constraints and pressures which is rarely one-sided and rarely simple.

Nonetheless, the point must be made in principle. A moral scalpel is still needed to expose all the potential ingredients of the situation, however opaque the moral state of any individual caught up in it. It is necessary to recognize and expose a false appeal to faithfulness. This will always be important for the moral credibility of a proper call to faithfulness – which must remain self-critical in all its limits and possibilities.

8

PRACTICES IN PERSONAL
RELATIONSHIPS

Faithfulness matters – but in what kinds of relationship does it matter most? The biblical covenant traditions set out its priorities. Our relationship with God is pre-eminent, the foundation of our human identity. Integral to that is our belonging to the community of the people of God. Covenant language is also used in individual personal relations. It is clearly related to marriage. Loyalty to wider family and kinship networks and to the state is largely assumed and sometimes taught. All these relationships bear on our identity, and become significant sites for faithfulness.

The selection of specific sites for discussion in the next two chapters is only partly determined by this biblical agenda. Space is a constraint. It is also a matter of methodology. First, there is the straightforward question of relevance. Whenever theology wants to speak publicly it must speak faithfully out of its own tradition, but it must also speak into the public situation as it is, not simply as it was in the origins of the tradition. So what follows is tangential to the biblical background. It selects two areas of social life which are in the current foreground of rapid change and which cause particular concern in our current sense of personal identity. The first – personal relationships including family life and marriage – was a clear part of the biblical agenda and remains critical in our world. The second – practices of working life – was not high on the agenda then, but it is now. The other reason for this selection is to concentrate on specifically social and ethical concerns. This is not meant to challenge the primacy of the religious concern. Faithfulness to God and the people of God remains foundational – a proper and deserving subject of much more discussion. The quick move here to social issues simply signals two other gospel priorities. First, it indicates the urgency of the evangelical concern already indicated: to address people where they are. Second, it embodies the theological principle that God is served through our social relationships, not in abstraction from them. To say how we might love God apart from how we love our brother and sister is to say something meaningless. It is the worst of all worlds. It neither comes out of the biblical tradition nor speaks into any contemporary situation.

Family, friendships, marriage: some recent observations

Social patterns within which kinship, family, friendship, marriage take shape and significance have always changed, but not always at the present rate of change. There have been periods of relative stability when societies were shaped by a common tradition which cemented and perpetuated social practices. This stability is self-reinforcing when strong kinship and family ties across generations are themselves effective transmitters of the very traditions which support them.[1] But in a post-traditional society such as ours there is neither the cohesion nor transmitting power of tradition to hold back the rate of change. In a post-Enlightenment culture where the control of scientific reason has provided no agreed alternative to tradition, the space for change opens up further. A post-industrial society of social mobility and globalization accelerates the process. It severs old allegiances by uprooting people from settled places.[2] In this context both the creation of ourselves and our relationships is largely devolved to personal choice and control. That further opens the floodgates of change. In these conditions of late-postmodernity the self constantly has to renew or refashion itself, incorporating new experience and knowledge. And it will do this either by itself or by calling in a huge variety of technical expertise (e.g.

therapy), rather than drawing on a settled and rooted tradition passed on from generation to generation. This ' reflexive project' of self-identity, as Giddens has called it, is an intrinsically dynamic process attempting to cope with an intrinsically dynamic context.[3]

This general context of change and disturbance has specific effects on human relationships. What is measurable in public practices is clear enough. In family life, marriage has decreased, the rate of divorce, single-parent families, absent fathers, non-marital births, and varied forms of cohabitation and sexual partnerships have all increased. These changes have been documented from various perspectives of the social sciences, and with different evaluations. Most early responses in the 1950s to 1970s described them in relatively positive terms. The changes offered liberation to women imprisoned in oppressive relationships. They were part of an economic and social empowerment, long overdue in this patriarchal society. To begin with there seemed little evidence that children suffered any particular harm. If there was damage to children, the main cause was reckoned to be poverty, not the changing structure of family life. Marriage itself was reckoned to intensify conflict and harm the most vulnerable members of the family. However, more recently there has been a shift in perception. Studies from the 1980s uncovered new forms of imprisonment suffered by women. Single mothers are just as likely to suffer economic and social exclusion as empowerment. Broken families and the absence of a father increased the likelihood of psychological, social, educational harm in children, even when the damaging effects of poverty are taken into account. The family in general and marriage in particular is considered a site where conflicts from wider social and psychological pressures must be accommodated, rather than the chief cause of those conflicts. The damage of extreme individualism is more readily noted and commitment in general has begun to be commended again, if not practised. This shift in perception is not uncontested, but cannot be ignored.[4]

What is not measurable, but just as significant, is the changing texture of our human relationships within these changing social practices. In these terms kinship relations are probably the least affected because they retain some 'external', given structure which is not subject to wholesale change. This is the basic structure of biological relatedness which generates a grid of practices involving mutual responsibilities and obligations. It is based on a kind of natural law of joint interests vested in the survival and flourishing of all who carry our genes. Children first, but also siblings and other blood relations, all come within this category. It is evident from common experience, but also critically confirmed within the discipline of evolutionary psychology.[5] Nonetheless, even this biological givenness is not immune from changing social and cultural construction, and deconstruction. The wider context of late modernity has loosened even these biological bonds and changed their significance. The root of the change is the way this context has made us all more self-referential. One obvious example of its effect is how the 'problematic' of care for the elderly has developed. The very fact that it is perceived to be a problem is significant. The problem is not just generated by longevity and the economics of providing long-term pensions; it is the problem that the self-referential person has with any given social role which involves long-term duty without obvious personal rewards. Because we now see ourselves reflexively, i.e. involved in shaping ourselves, all our relationships are reviewed in that light. None is simply given to us along with its appropriate role: instead, we bring to all our relationships an element of participation, choice, commitment, *according to its effect on ourselves*. This makes our participation and commitment negotiable, even in kinship relations. The very fact that it is negotiable in this way makes it, precisely, problematic – in a way that would not be recognizable in many premodern societies.

What appears partially in kinship relationships is much more evident in other kinds of relationships. Where constraints of biological connection do not exist, and where the social and moral practices of tradition have been dissolved, the changed texture of relationships becomes, in Giddens's term, quite 'pure'. That is, it is understood through the dynamics of the relationship itself, rather than through wider social, economic or external moral criteria. This is most obviously the case in close friendships, sexual partnerships and marriage. The main features of these relationships for the late-modern self can be characterized like this. It means there is a strong element of choice and commitment. But this will sustain the relationship only as long as satisfaction obtains for those involved, or at least as long as the cost of withdrawing is not greater than persisting. In Giddens's analysis, commitment becomes central because it replaces the external anchors of social role, tradition, economic necessity, and it 'buys time' through difficult or unrewarding periods. But it can never be unconditional precisely because it is a matter of choice in a relationship which exists only for the sake of its own (unreliable) rewards. Giddens also highlights the element of risk and trust involved. Trust has to be achieved through the dynamics of a risky relationship. This follows from any relationship which is negotiable, not given. It is also the particular consequence of living with the reflexive self of late modernity. For if we are engaged in endless self-examination and self-creation then a relationship can only be sustained through trust that the changes can be accommodated. When obsessive reflexivity precipitates radical change then the risk is higher – and the relationship easily shattered. These relationships are also textured by a quest for great intimacy. This is a consequence of diminished roles and meaning elsewhere in a post-traditional society, and the depersonalizing effects of globalization, displacement and change itself. In such a world the personal relations which are chosen and intimate become a site of intense meaning and potential satisfaction. They are pivotal in fulfilling or fracturing our sense of personal identity. They bear a huge weight of expectation and disappointment. After breakdown, the renewed search for a new and 'truer' relationship is another symptom of the significance we attach to such intimate relationships. They matter for who we are much more than received social roles.

Evaluating the changes and Christian perspectives

One marked shift in the evaluation of these changes has been noted already. The 'objective' circumstances of broken homes and absent fathers have increasingly been judged harmful to children, and not always a liberation for women. This needs amplifying. First, as it relates to children. It now seems that single- or step-parent families *generally* disadvantage children, even when social disapproval is replaced by acceptance and economic support is adequate. Stable and biologically related fathers provide significant socializing and emotional ingredients in the nurture of children, and their absence is keenly felt. This view is now a major trend, particularly in American research where the process of family change has been monitored over a long period.[6] None of this ignores the evident damage done by poor parenting by either mother or father, whether biologically related or not. It makes no judgement against particular circumstances in which single parenthood is either imposed or chosen in preference to (for example) a violent father. It is simply an attempt to evaluate the relative effect of stability, shared parenthood and biological relatedness over against instability, single and step-parenthood, all other things being equal. Don Browning offers this judicious summary of the research, reasons for its findings, and its implications:

> Although biological relatedness does not guarantee good parenting by either mother or father, it seems to be a pre-moral . . . good that encourages parental investment and therefore correlates positively with moral qualities such as commitment, presence, steadfastness and positive regard – qualities which are directly related to child flourishing. As a pre-moral good, it is not to be absolutized but held as a relative good to be encouraged . . . *there should* [therefore] *be a presumption towards encouraging the formation and maintenance of intact families.*[7]

This position of holding the 'intact' family in high esteem for the sake of children is argued on the grounds of general social morality: it is for their flourishing. It also resonates for Browning and others on specifically Christian grounds. Admittedly, biblical traditions are not straightforward about this. They do not provide much explicit support for connecting marriage and a stable family structure to the well-being of children. But it is implicit in the kinship narratives, in the high valuation (though not sentimentality[8]) put on children in the Gospels, on the right ordering of households in the Epistles, and the injunction to fathers to nurture their children in their spiritual inheritance.[9] The developing Christian tradition gives a similar kind of support. It does not always speak with one voice. As we have seen, there is continuing theological tussle with Pauline 'concessionary' texts which grudge marriage and sexuality, and with Gnostic and Manichaean attitudes to sexual and family life. Nonetheless, this background of opposition to family life did not prevent another more dominant Augustinian tradition emerging. In this, children become an explicit 'good' of marriage, linked with faith itself, for the sake of whom marriage must be deemed indissoluble.[10] A recent review of this tradition, although working in a postmodern and liberal context, has drawn out from it clear foundations for a renewed and robust theology of 'liberation for children'.[11]

For women the evaluative shift commands less consensus. The experience of oppression within patriarchal forms of marriage has scarred women, not only in relation to men but in their relation to motherhood. It has made it hard for some to accept any reconstructed notion of marriage-based family life. The institution of marriage itself has seemed irredeemably contaminated. Nonetheless, a positive reconstruction is taking place. A key principle is to strip away all patriarchal practices and prejudices, economic, emotional and social, so that parenthood is truly shared. In this way women may be fulfilled rather than exploited in their motherhood, as in their other roles.[12] Another principle is to involve wider networks of kinship beyond the so-called nuclear family. These will support or even share the parenting of children, particularly in the socializing of children in a wider community. This too means a potential enrichment rather than oppression of a woman's identity within marriage. Again, this draws from Christian tradition and reflection, as well as from the wider moral reflections of secular feminists. It is widely accepted that biblical traditions of patriarchy have acted to fossilize marriage roles in oppressive structures: but alongside this there has always been an underlying egalitarian *direction* in the biblical stories. It is signalled by Jesus' gospel attitudes to women and the Epistles' occasional bolts from the eschatological blue.[13] This trajectory has now eventually found its *kairos*, not in the most radical deconstructions of early Christian feminists but in their more recent reconstructions of family life which want women to be fulfilled within them, not in spite of them. The tradition has now reached a position where a Christian feminist can affirm a woman's role in an 'ideal family'. There is no return here to the suggestion that a woman *must* be a mother. But there is reappropriation of female identity (including bodily identity) which *can* be fulfilled in a situation where

> both biological parents nurture children physically and emotionally, and educate them by example for larger social roles; in which parents and children are supported by a 'kin' network; and in which parents are fulfilled not only through sexually expressed love for each other, but through mutual and equal dedication to offspring, to family, and to the larger community.[14]

All this suggests a firm Christian response to changes in the public practice of human relationships in marriage, family and parenthood. The present trajectory of instability, single and step-parenthood, is often harmful to children and has even become counterproductive for the liberation of women. It also fails more generally to meet our personal and social needs for flourishing. In Browning's terms, it calls for a presumption in favour of intact families. It is a view which does not depend solely on theological insights, but connects readily with wider public concern. It is the kind of response which can also be seen in some recent Church reports. For example, the general social goods of stable marriage and family life, and their specific value for children, are stressed in the Church of England report *Something to Celebrate*. This is not based solely on the reiteration of traditional teaching. It is expressed as a real engagement of that tradition with current realities. It is precisely to meet the needs of fractured personal identity and social instability that more stable, though dynamic, patterns of family life need to be reaffirmed.[15]

So much for the observable practices. But how do we evaluate the more general underlying changes? What are we to make of the inner texture of relationships?

The brief picture already offered portrays late-modern relationship as complex and paradoxical. Giddens's summary suggests something both potent and fragile, self-satisfying and self-destructive, morally commendable and morally dubious. So how can we analyse it further to evaluate it better?

The potency of our close human relationships lies in the intimacy, significance and emotional depth they offer in an impersonal, mobile, globalized world. In this world, where neither place, community or tradition can command such intimacy, our chosen personal relationships provide it with greater and greater intensity. This 'sequestering' of experience, as Giddens calls it, has much the same effect as MacIntyre's earlier analysis of the self in a society dominated by instrumental reason. It separates the self-in-relationship from other potential sources of existential and moral significance which exist as discrete systems of expertise (at work, in virtual reality, in technology, medicine etc.). This sets up a divided self, torn between the values of different roles unrelated within any overall story. But above all it intensifies the drive to seek refuge in the close human relationships which we choose.

The fragility of such relationships is the reverse side of this intensity and sense of refuge which they provide. They are being made to bear too much weight on their own. As such a primary source of meaning and self-identity, they easily implode. Psychologically they tend to over-dependence which then stifles the restless 'reflexive' drive to change, self-expression, self-creation, and creates frustration and dissatisfaction. Socially they are cut off from a wider framework of shared meaning which could provide the space to grow together, rather than stifle each other. Moreover, that potential support of a wider framework of meaning is itself spurious. The wider framework we actually encounter is not a supporting tradition. As Giddens points out, the same impersonal, mobile, globalized context which drives us into intimate human relationships also forces us to connect with other 'systems' of life. We live within worlds of employment, shopping, education, training, the media. These worlds all bring other people, roles, lifestyles into our view. They present themselves as alternatives, options to draw on to help us out of dissatisfaction. But these 'authorities' are no longer the authorities of a tradition or family structure which draw from a common moral world to hold us *within* a relationship. They are discontinuous and potentially disruptive worlds which are just as likely to tempt us out of our existing relationships. Therapy can operate in this way, by encouraging self-determination out of the resources of an individual's own life story rather than any shared tradition. It presents itself as a system of expertise to be drawn in from outside a relationship to help it, but may have the effect of heightening its inner dissatisfactions.[16]

So how do we evaluate this? What do we make of the relationships at the heart of it all? It is not always easy to see their moral strengths. Intensity and fragility are not a promising context for satisfying relationships. Nonetheless, there are significant moral values at stake. The fact that relationships are largely chosen rather than inherited requires a kind of commitment and trust which creates the potential for new dimensions of moral responsibility. We have already noted that trust has to be earned and achieved through the quality of the relationship, rather than assumed by virtue of a 'given' role. The responsibility of working out relationships by mutual consent rather than received practices may impose pressure but it also pushes us to explore deeper levels of reciprocity and empathy. So, at best, the reflexive and self-examining self could actually encourage mutual and constructive change. In principle it can contemplate what Brummer advocates: creative change in itself in order to accommodate its partner's change. For the same reason it can encourage the constructive contemplation of the future. If we are to continue to choose and enjoy an intimate relationship then the future consequences of present actions and attitudes have to be more responsibly weighed. This is in contrast to the relationship of a given role in which the future itself seems fixed and needs less thought.

But of course the moral dangers are compelling too. They emerge as a clear correlate to what is positive. These relationships are made out of reflexive selves who are *choosing* a commitment. But on what basis? The problems here have been hinted at already. Selves who are isolated from wider traditions and only concerned with choice, self-assessment, self-creation, will choose a relationship which depend on self-satisfaction and rewards internal to that relationship. Moreover, the measure of that satisfaction can only be derived ultimately from the self in that relationship, not even from the relationship per se. So the determining question of the relationship reduces to 'What does it mean for me?' It has been described as a culture of narcissism.[17] The individual has been reduced by the pressures of modernity to a moral paucity and passivity which can only draw strength from itself. This will inevitably destroy relationship. Any will to change in accordance with a partner's change is sapped by the overriding imperative to preserve and satisfy oneself. Any effort to accommodate the relationship in the future is dismissed as greater than the effort of ending the relationship. Its immediate effect within relationships is disastrous. Searching for intimacy but forced to maintain its own survival and self-creation, the self demands more and more from its partner but cannot give anything of itself away. This bleak analysis of the experience of reflexive selves in so-called 'pure relationship' is an extreme view.[18] But the general dynamics of it can be widely seen at work. Even if each partner is not individually narcissistic to such a dangerous degree, the relationship itself may exhibit some of these characteristics. It is likely to be introverted and unable to give itself away. By existing chiefly for themselves within a relationship existing for itself, partners will be unable to integrate children properly within the relationship or incorporate wider kinship and social responsibilities. It is a long way from Cahill's ideal family.

This does not imply a wholly negative evaluation. The sheer complexity of human nature and human relationships means that positive features are often embedded in the negative, and vice versa. The shifting nature of empirical evidence may also present new perspectives. In a social context which encourages self-regarding short-term relationships, the evidence of damaged children, stress and inter-generational irresponsibility is certainly a powerful indication of moral bankruptcy. But other empirical data can qualify this. Giddens draws heavily on work by Judith Stacey to make the point. From research carried out in Silicon Valley she shows how

> individuals are actively re-structuring new forms of gender and kinship relation out of the detritus of pre-established forms of family life . . . divorce is being mobilised as a resource to create networks drawing together new partners and former ones, biological children and stepchildren, friends and other relatives. *Narcissism is not a trait which emerges with any clarity from such studies as Stacey's where individuals appear not as withdrawing from the outer social world but engaging boldly with it.*[19]

This offers a morally encouraging answer to the cautious query of a 1990 Church Report: 'we do not yet know what loyalty there may be to estranged in-laws or step-parents'. [20] It suggests a more positive evaluation of the inner texture of relationships as well as public practice of them. Of itself it does not reverse the general evaluative shift with which we began. But it is a sign of a complex moral resilience in human agency which belies social determinism and subverts easy moral judgements. We must not oversimplify.

So what of traditional Christian perspectives? Will they be more decisive guides for our inner relationships? Not easily. This is partly because the reflexive self-conscious scrutiny of ourselves in our relationships is generally considered an invention of modernity. It means there is not much direct biblical reflection on the inner texture of such relationships. For example, marriage and sexual partnership are mostly considered as public practice. The inner dynamics and private feelings are not a chief concern. Thus the lifelong union of man and woman portrayed in Genesis seems to be given chiefly as a divine ordinance of creation, not as an existential fulfilment of individuals. Jesus' endorsement of it in the Gospels re-establishes it on those terms. The fact that the one flesh union is represented as being for friendship (not specifically for procreation) hints at elements of 'pure' relationship – but the inner landscape of relationship is not really explored. Likewise, when Jesus pronounces on divorce, his reported concerns are not primarily with the inner dynamics of the relationship. Instead he appears to be positioning himself theologically in relation to various Rabbinic schools, maintaining the creation tradition but allowing exceptions, possibly to protect women's social or economic position.[21] Similarly, the prophets' use of marriage in covenant language is not necessarily a good guide. They refer to passion, trust, betrayal – but the terms are used chiefly for the main task of teaching the right (collective) relationship of a people with Yahweh, rather than the dynamics of individual personal relations.

Yet this is not the whole story. It would be a modern conceit to deny *any* premodern concern for the dynamics of personal relationships. There may not have been the reflexive intensity of modernity, but there was still some sense of personal sensibility, something not entirely determined by social role. There are some biblical signposts to this. When the Epistle to the Ephesians refers to the analogy of Christ's self-giving relationship to the Church it suggests real inner dispositions in marriage relationships. The concern for the husband to love his wife's body *as his own self* suggests a profound inner exchange of self-giving.[22] Moreover, these inner dynamics of relationship seem to be given weight over against purely social roles. For while the initiating shape of the analogy may have been patriarchal, its development is far from it. It is potentially subversive of the patriarchal structure precisely by appeal to the dynamics of the relationship. In this way it begins to transcend the predominant patriarchal roles which shaped the 'external' practices.

What evaluation is then given to this sort of relationship? It is twofold. It certainly endorses some of the inner freedom of modern 'pure' relationship. But it also uses that freedom in a distinctive way. It is the freedom of mutual self-giving and sacrifice rather than the narcissistic drive to self-gratification. It accepts the form of current dispositions, but clearly opposes much of their current content.

There is also concern for the personal interior life in the Sermon on the Mount. Inner attitudes of lust, anger, evil thoughts matter, not just public behaviour which flouts an external law of behaviour. Forgiveness and loving an enemy matter more than enforcing a law of retribution. It is perverse to believe Jesus only taught this to establish a theological position for himself in a conflict of religious authority. It surely expresses at least some concern for the inner shape of the soul – which then bears on all kinds of relationships. It is not pressed home in specific terms (e.g. of a marriage relationship or other close friendship), but is clearly intended as a general pattern for neighbour-love. Much the same must be said of Paul's eulogy of love which is 'patient, kind . . . does not insist on its own way . . . is not resentful, does not rejoice in wrongdoing . . . bears all things, believes all things, hopes all things, endures all things'.[23] The main context is discipleship and relationships within the Church, rather than the modern arena of intimate partnerships. But it still articulates a spiritual and moral map for other human relationships, with or without the given parameters of a strong social role.

The evaluation suggested by this map again has a twofold thrust. It is a map which implies some sense of choice in a freely given commitment, and that is valued. Equally, because it is always based on the free initiative of God's love for us (in

Johannine terms, love 'as I have loved you'), that free commitment is to be unconditional, long-term self-giving – not the contingent, shifting, self-creating commitment of the modern self.

Subsequent theological reflection on the nature of this *agape* love offers much the same judgement. It includes some endorsement of chosen commitment, self-involvement, trust, and freedom. For example, it has recently re-emphasized the element of self-fulfilment within the process of self-giving. It has modified the most austere Protestant readings of Augustine to allow self-love and need-love to find some place within other-love and gift love: *eros* finds some place within *agape*. This connects with some of the concerns of late modernity. Equally, it presents a radical challenge to the self-referential texture of modern relationships, particularly its tendency to narcissism and short-term contingency. So the critique from the Gospel remains sharp: such self-fulfilment can only be attained through radical and unconditional self-giving.[24] In these ways we can evaluate where we are – and where we need to go. Some clear moral comment *is* possible, even though experience is complex.

The disposition of faithfulness

But because it remains an area of genuine and shifting complexity in which disparate moral comment may not always be adequate, this again raises the question of a co-ordinating moral *disposition*. And when we look for such a disposition to guide us through this particular moral maze, 'faithfulness' again proves invaluable. In its full Christian sense it is a compelling notion here as in other areas. It will be both realistic and radical. It is not a revisionist grid to stamp on the scene to force it back into some premodern mould – we could not do that even if it was wanted. It will be able to accommodate changing roles, conflicting loyalties, responsibility to others, as well the fulfilment of our own personal identity. It will be able to recognize the mixed evaluation of late modernity – both to affirm its best goals and avoid its worst dangers. But for all that, it will help hold us within our relationships through time and change.

In this field of personal relationships it will operate with a very clear presumption. In all these relationships of marriage, family, kinship, faithfulness summons us *to keep the covenant created by the roles*. This matters as much with what Anthony Harvey calls the covenant across the generations as with the marriage covenant.[25] It is therefore a presumption which requires us to inhabit a whole narrative of time with our children, our parents and grandparents, as well as our marriage partners. To stay with them through the changes and chances of life will help fulfil both their identity and our own. At the same time, this will not depend on unrealistically fixed roles or unchanging personality. When there is change – from child to parent, from breadwinner to housekeeper, from self-sufficiency to dependency, from introvert to extrovert, malleable to assertive – the meaning of faithfulness is to change responsively within the relationship, rather than cut and run from the relationship itself. This is the natural trajectory of a faithful disposition and character which accommodates the contingencies of role or personality without being wholly defined by them.

In this disposition there is space for what modernity has celebrated. It does not deny the existential and moral values of freedom, choice, commitment, trust. We are not just required to practise the public duties imposed by the roles of kinship and other family relationships. We are invited in to appropriate their inner dynamics. That is what the call for responsive change allows and demands. Within close friendships and marriage partnerships faithfulness permits radical choice and risk at the outset, then requires the sustained exercise of responsive commitment throughout the relationship. So the late-modern quest for self-review and self-creation is not suppressed: responsive change within a relationship actually requires a reflexive self. But at the same time faithfulness requires a critique of the self within these relationships. The element of self-creation must not be in a purely self-referential framework. It must not seek 'authenticity' or self-satisfaction simply out of the immediate framework of the present state of a relationship. Instead it must be self-creation within the long narrative of the relationship and a wider connected set of relationships. Faithfulness reminds us that our own identity is fulfilled by looking to the whole narrative well-being of the other person and the wider web of the changing relationships which form their identity. So it has to 'colonize' the future and take account of wider society within the experience of the relationship.

In this way the presumption of faithfulness provides a clear moral framework, and within that it offers its own rewards. By binding us to our relationships it holds us to a much richer definition of personal identity than the appeal to a passing sense of 'personal authenticity' or 'self-satisfaction'. Modernity's great prize of freedom and goal of self-discovery is not denied but radically redirected. Put in other terms, we may still find our life, but only if we lose it – in faithfulness. The basis for this is worth repeating. It lies in both the theology and the general anthropology already set out. We are unitary beings who thread our way through time and change, however much the change we experience in circumstance, role, or personality. This continuity of personhood is a critical foundation for our overall identity. It is secured theologically by God's creating and sustaining love, but also recognized by some secular anthropologies. It therefore makes ontological as well as moral sense to respect this continuity in our relationships in and through the processes of change. The call to faithfulness is grounded in the way things are, as well as vindicated by the evidence of current social experience. That is why it can bring satisfaction when it is practised. It is why both children and adults are damaged when it is abandoned.

Hard cases

But how does this overall presumption work in the hardest of cases? How can it operate when damage is done not by abandoning a relationship, but by the dynamics within a relationship? What happens when roles conflict destructively?

We need to recall the discussion of previous chapters. First, a presumption related to a disposition of character does not generate a precise hierarchy of rules. It invites modes of behaviour arising out of consistent attitudes. So the call to faithfulness in itself will not decide on every particular issue of personal relations. For example, it cannot tell us in every case whether care for an ageing parent with dementia should take precedence over time spent with a demanding young family. It cannot decide whether a particular marriage has become irredeemably destructive, whether divorce is the only option. There is a proper theological and ecclesiastical discussion to be undertaken about guidelines for divorce and remarriage – but that is not the task of this kind of theological ethics.

Nonetheless, this kind of approach will offer more general guidance. It will insist that faithfulness must be allowed full play, even in difficult circumstances. As Farley showed, hard cases press commitment to find new ways to express itself. The presumption of faithfulness must not be foreclosed. It must be allowed to exert its full pressure. So modes of behaviour and difficult decisions will arise out of this consistent disposition, even though they cannot be specifically legislated in advance.

For example, a consistent presumption of faithfulness will not allow us to sideline the claims of an elderly relative, or abandon a marriage relationship, *simply* on the grounds of changed personality. The objective role remains and the meaning of faithfulness will try to incorporate change within that role, not cut and run from it. In hard and tragic cases where personality change is accompanied by persistent destructive behaviour (paranoia, violence) the role may eventually have to change. But in this case faithfulness still has to be fulfilled in some other way – the most likely way is to find others to take over a role of direct responsibility (such as professional help to care for the sick or demented). And even in these cases it is not change itself which will have justified the radical change of role, only a behavioural pattern which makes it impossible to perform the role. This was the point made earlier: role and responsibility end, or are changed, only when an agent is rendered causally incapable of fulfilling it, even when she is willing to change herself. In other words it only completely ends when there is a kind of death.

Even then it does not die easily. Because the full meaning of faithfulness extends beyond the present moment to the whole narrative identity of the other person, it need not wholly end even when roles change. A consistent character of faithfulness will continue to exercise appropriate responsibility wherever it can. For example, there will be a presumption of loyalty to the wider web of relations which still constitute the parent's or partner's identity, even after dementia, death or divorce. This is often worked out instinctively in the new forms of extended loyalty to step-families, in-laws of divorced partners, and other friends – the sort of response charted by Stacey's research in Silicon Valley. This is how a presumption of faithfulness operates when it has been deep-rooted in character. It is almost never exhausted because it will instinctively seek new ways of expressing itself, rather than a way out of itself. Unlike a deontological ethic of precise rules, it does not become instantly inapplicable when circumstances change. It does not offer the easy escape of casuistry.

Faithfulness and reciprocity

In this way it becomes clear that reciprocity is not a necessary condition of the disposition of faithfulness. This marks a difference between dispositions and relations, and further explains the added meaning that faithfulness gives to love. McFadyen rightly insists that 'a real relation cannot, by definition, be assured from one side alone'[26] – which in turn means that reciprocity is bound to be vital for the specific relation of love.[27] This is widely accepted: love defined as a relationship cannot be fully expressed unilaterally but depends on a freely given exchange between partners to be itself. It is why my continuing 'love' for a separated or departed person who cannot return it easily reduces from a rewarding relationship to a frustrated attitude. It may remain morally valuable, even heroic, but it offers no appropriate behavioural outlet. That is also why the outcome of unrequited love can be damaging self-imprisonment. It locks the lover in the past, the present is empty, and the future can only be appropriated through fantasy. But it is another matter with faithfulness. The disposition and behavioural patterns of faithfulness do not depend on existential reciprocity. When a faithful relationship can no longer be performed reciprocally, the regret and the devastation may be the same as unrequited love, but the disposition of faithfulness retains its meaning and purpose. It can find new ways of expressing faithfulness, even if this entails new roles. And this will fulfil our identity just as much as the old ways which have been closed off by change and circumstance.

Almost every parent–child relationship experiences this. As a child grows up to leave parents and cleave to other loyalties there are stages where reciprocity is profoundly affected, often diminished. But good parents do not stop being parents. They instinctively search for new modes of behaviour to express their faithfulness and their identity as parents. In one way or another they try actively to be 'there' for their children, whatever distance has opened up. This is a complex process. It is driven partly by the given biological continuities of the parents' role but also involves enforced role changes within the overall 'master-role' of parenthood. It may be partly motivated by the prospect of renewed reciprocity later in the relationship but it has no guarantee of it. It remains nonetheless a process of change within which faithfulness is maintained and has its proper modes of behaviour. The same may be said when a faithful child seeks different ways to continue caring for an ageing parent who requires professional care. It can be said when a divorced partner continues to take some responsibility for step-children or in-laws. The emotional complexities of displaced guilt and resentments are huge, and often make these modes of faithful behaviour desperately hard to perform. Yet they still can and do flow from a character of faithfulness. Faithfulness is being expressed in whatever way is practically and psychologically possible, even when there is no obvious reciprocity.

This claim that even 'frustrated' faithfulness can fulfil our identity is not always easy to sustain. But it may help to recall the initial definitions of personhood. A definition of personhood which reduced simply to the reciprocity of relations could not readily sustain this disposition. McFadyen's discussion of fidelity seems to bear this out. While he values fidelity and agrees that 'genuine personhood is derived from fidelity' he also has to say that the identities of partners require the *'mutuality* of trust and fidelity'.[28] He is bound to say this on the basis of his own wholly relational definition of personhood. However, if we assume the notion of an enduring personhood which is not wholly relational, then it becomes easier to accept that reciprocity does not have the power of veto. We can demonstrate that there *is* meaning in the unrequited disposition of faithfulness – which is dynamic, not merely dogged, and which genuinely fulfils our identity. Another way is simply to recall the divine model. What we saw to be true of divine faithfulness must also be true for ours. The experience of reciprocity is not all. The elements of initiative and unconditionality which are so clear in the divine disposition must be echoed in ours. Covenants of human faithfulness must try to draw on the divine covenant. It is another mark of faithfulness which takes us beyond at least some notions of love.

Of course, this does not mean there is no reciprocity at a more profound level. By being faithful we are, precisely, fulfilling our personal identity. That is in itself a form of reciprocity. It is a matter of fact even when we experience no immediate satisfactions in return. This follows from the anthropology we have adopted, where personal identity means more than current experience. This means there may be all sorts of satisfactions to follow at some stage – as already suggested. Nor are they always wholly hidden or endlessly deferred. They surface in the unique qualities of joy evident in many faithful relationships, particularly in long-term marriage, parenthood, grandparenthood. But they are not cheaply or easily won. They are not susceptible to the superficial empiricism of late-modernity, its empirical *impatience*. This is the sharp end of the theological critique of modernity. Theological faithfulness is an article of faith because empirical data can never wholly confirm it. It is a situation when we sometimes have to make do with merely negative evidence: we can only observe the empirical effects of the *absence* of faithfulness. This was the point with which we began. Where the icon of faithfulness has been lost in late modernity we reap the outcome in our troubled sense of self and society, and faith believes there will be corresponding benefits if the icon is restored. But it cannot always show them. In short, we may often have to live *as if* there is no reciprocity – whatever the final truth of the matter.

Recovering an icon

But how do we live it? How can we set out in practice to recover faithfulness in human relationships – with or without instant satisfactions? Theology or the churches cannot undertake this task alone. To create character requires a narrative tradition and a plausibility structure to sustain it. This is a tall order in a plural and fluid world which is still wary of meta-narrative, and the churches alone will not succeed. The ecclesial response of withdrawal in order to create a 'community of character' sealed off from the pressures of pluralism in the wider world might just succeed. But this is ultimately unacceptable because it is an expression of sectarianism. It could not fulfil the theological imperative to be the body of Christ in and for God's whole world. It could be justified as a temporary strategy with the ultimate purpose of witnessing more effectively to the wider world: *reculer pour mieux sauter*, in the MacIntyrean sense, in the way that Christian faith and practice clung on in the Celtic fringes of the British Isles in the Dark Ages before recolonizing the mainland.[29] Yet even this strategy could not stand alone for long. Theology and the Church must always be serving the world as well as themselves. Incarnation, sacrament, mission are intrinsically relational and embodied notions. They wither without full expression 'outwards'. So the character of faithfulness must always be expressed externally in public policy as well as internally in church order – and it will look for the help of public partners.

However, in so far as the internal dimension still matters –

as part of this wider mission – it will set a clear agenda. The whole ecclesial project of building a settled, liturgically ordered 'community of character' in a particular place will remain vital. It is a context of stability in which loyalty and faithfulness will be embedded. It will be an important axis of continuity in the disturbances of late-postmodern life which tend to sever place, time and community. In particular, it will include specific areas of pastoral and practical concern. For example, it will require greater discipline in all marriage preparation, and it will require divorcees to include particular kinds of preparation before remarriage. All will have to learn ways of expressing faithfulness without reciprocity. This will need to be expressed liturgically in a rite of remarriage which does not merely repeat the first marriage. Instead it must recognize how the narrative of a life has moved on, but incorporate these new demands that faithfulness makes of the past as well as the future. In addition, there must be practical support for marriage and all intergenerational relationships by networks of care from the wider church family. The practices of nursery playgroups, youth groups, pastoral visiting schemes, need to be structured by this priority. This means that youth work will not just take young people off their parents' hands for an evening a week. It will actively involve the parents in the whole narrative of young people's lives, and vice versa. In the same way pastoral visits of the elderly will not be isolated but integrated by contact with the lives of their families. In other words, the 'professionalism' which keeps clear boundaries in aspects of pastoral care needs to be complemented by crossing boundaries in moral and spiritual care.

But of course the external agenda of this theology stretches a long way beyond church order and practices. It will require a sustained mission of general public support for commitment and faithfulness. This means changing the stories people live by. Public culture will have to be changed through reshaping the role models of soap operas and the media presentation of public figures in entertainment, sport, politics. Media stories in particular will connect widely because there is a wistfulness for satisfying sub-narratives (in spite of suspicion of metanarratives). The sub-narratives embodied in church life and local community organizations may help: but in a globalized, mobile, and virtual world of communication they must be embodied in the media as well. The external agenda will also include reform of some specific social policies. It will require adequate tax benefits for married couples. It will also press for financial support to sustain *any* long-term commitment: single parents needs a structure of support to sustain their parental commitment effectively, just as much as married couples. In the long term there is the question of housing provision. This must be proactive, even if it means breaking out of the constraint of market forces. The priority is to build multi-roomed houses to help realize the goal of wider and longer-term family commitments, rather than reinforcing current trends to solitary living and smaller households.

More general attitudes and these specific policies will both matter, for a moral call to faithfulness – as with any moral shift – is only likely to enter effectively into such a mobile social structure by its embodiment at every level. This is the challenge of transforming a vicious circle to a virtuous circle. An ever increasing disintegration of the self and its relationships will not be reintegrated by a single catalyst. Character requires a wider field of nurture, and both Church and wider society must be involved in providing it. Only then will the lost icon of faithfulness in personal relationships begin to find its way back, as it badly needs to, in a redeeming way.

9

PRACTICES OF WORK

Many other sites of faithfulness, particularly in our social life and structures, deserve consideration. Ethnic belonging is an important example. It is a telling area. It generates fierce loyalties, often intensified by overlapping religious allegiance. It deserves attention, especially in the light of current conflicts. It involves a particularly dense interrelation of religious and political issues, however, and needs more than a final chapter. The principles of faithfulness I have outlined will apply, but discussion of specific practices would require another book.

Another obvious arena is political allegiance. The overall structure of relations between the state, governments and peoples has always demanded some sort of mutual loyalty. Long before the Enlightenment notion of social contract there were other kinds of contract and covenant. That is why questions of 'state' authority naturally emerge from the biblical narrative, even if they are not dominant. Post-Enlightenment history has shaped these questions of political philosophy and theology in different ways, but it has not abandoned them.[1] In this area justice is often the co-ordinating moral notion, rather than loyalty, but covenant faithfulness is again a ready handmaid. Thus Clinton Gardner in *Justice and Christian Ethics*: 'It is of the nature and essence of every society to be knit together by some covenant, either expressed or implied.'[2] 'Covenant points to the fundamental unity of virtue and law in a concept of community and, more especially, of political community based upon mutual trust and fidelity to a common cause.'[3] But this area is ground well covered by others, and again deserves more discussion than a single chapter could provide.

A more specific area within social life might, however, benefit from a more limited discussion. There is the particular matter of our working culture and practices. It falls within general concerns of social order but has a specific shape within that. It has received some attention in discussions of the wider socio-economic context: Peter Sedgwick's work is a recent example which also deals with the general effect of this context on human identity.[4] But there is more to be said, particularly if working practices are scrutinized more specifically in relation to identity and *loyalty*. It is a significant field for enquiry because the intensity of personal experience generated in working lives is now more widespread and profound than our general experience of political life. In much Western/Northern culture it shapes personal identity in a more immediate way for many people than issues of national or political belonging. It is an important site for faithfulness.

Work and identity: a brief history

The extent to which work matters for human identity varies across time, culture and circumstance. But it always had some such role. It is a continuous thread through a great deal of our heritage and history. In the biblical traditions of Christian faith it is not a major theme: human significance is far from being solely constituted by our work, as Karl Barth amongst others has emphasized.[5] But it features nonetheless. The foundational biblical stories of creation root some sense of work in the creative being of God himself. It also belongs to the ideal 'Man' in Eden (Adam and Eve). In the fallen world work continues with this creative potential, although it also becomes a drudgery and a toilsome necessity. It has, as Ronald Preston says, a 'double aspect . . . as toil and joy'.[6] The New Testament briefly sanctifies it, almost in passing, as a vocation or 'calling', juxtaposed with the calling to discipleship – so although the call to discipleship is mostly worked out in other ways, work is not excluded.[7] Overall this is a more positive attitude to work than Greek traditions – where productive labour carried

a socially degrading status. It certainly suggests some sort of
constitutive role for work in human identity.

These biblical roots have been variously appropriated in the
developing tradition. In the traditional pre-industrial society
of Western christendom the agricultural context of work was
integrated with Christian identity in the liturgical cycles of the
Church. In the commercial world of work there were at least
some Church teachings (e.g. on usury) which recognized the
significance of working practices for moral and spiritual
identity. Work was a natural dimension of identity in this
period where occupation and social role were indistinguish-
able – though the positive notion of a specific *vocation* to work
was largely lost in the medieval tendency to reserve 'higher'
meanings of vocation to the explicitly religious life.

This issue was sharpened, as so often, in the ferment of
the religious Reformation and the dawning Enlightenment
period. Luther wanted to reinstate the equal value of vocation
for all. The notion of vocation 'was brought from the monas-
tery to the marketplace'.[8] What followed was the creative but
contentious and paradoxical relationship between Protestant
teaching and the growing economic dynamics of capitalism,
documented seminally by Weber. The main thesis remains
persuasive. A sense of divine command to pursue a vocation
at work wholeheartedly, combined with a Christian duty of
austerity, proved a powerful catalyst both to generate capital
and to develop rigorous efficiency in working practices. This
created the conditions in which the efficiency of work and the
market could eventually be accorded its own moral and
even spiritual status. It justified itself as a means of producing
wealth by harnessing the spiritual energies of vocation to
the energies of self-interest. This in turn was followed by the
burgeoning ethic of mass consumption which replaced the
original ethic of personal frugality. In the course of this
work now ceased to be the expression of an integrated
Christian identity and became the sphere in which another
sort of identity was being constructed, with different roles and
values. This was one of the main reasons for growing fragmentation of identity. It is an ironic development where the

outcome of the religious basis to identity at work is at odds with its original aspirations.

This account is still highly influential, although contested.[9] It certainly remains persuasive in the way it demonstrates the general significance of work for personal identity. This was a critical point in Marx's critique of capitalism. He saw the increasing division of labour which accompanied the rise of capitalism and industrialization as a threat both to personal freedom and social solidarity – both vital constituents of personal identity. Durkheim thought otherwise: division of labour could provide a unifying focus to identity by reducing 'the malady of infinite aspirations'. But both Marx and Durkheim, along with many others, agree in accepting the fundamental importance of working practices in the expression or construction of identity, for better or worse.

Such significance has been questioned or sidelined in more recent critical theorizing. Postmodern preoccupation with how cultural 'signs' create identity – particularly consumer identity – has pushed aside earlier concern about the effect of the means of production and other working practices. The sign replaces the commodity and the world of media communication replaces the workplace as the source of significance. The dynamics of the overall 'virtual' economic world becomes more significant for human identity than immediate wage-labour relations. For example, the general shift from a mass production economy to a consumer-driven economy intensifies the experience of personal choice. The ready availability of credit pressed on us by banks and other financial institutions, reinforced by media lifestyle images, gives more responsibility for decision-making to more 'ordinary' people. It shifts the discourse of the self from duty to the family or the future to desire for new self-image.[10]

This is a useful reminder of the wider cultural, social and economic context in which identity is affected, and which is Peter Sedgwick's main concern. Sedgwick is also particularly concerned to point out the ambivalence of this consumer-driven economy. The possibilities it provides for creating a new self-image can be a positive exercise of imagination, freedom and self-transcendence. Equally, by stimulating a desire for endless novelty it exposes a fragile self-image and threatened identity.[11] This echoes some of Giddens's observations about changing patterns of human relationships. But none of this means that work itself has ceased to be significant for identity. As Catherine Casey insists, work is itself a cultural practice and a site of cultural signs. The material conditions of a workplace and its practices and products still form a cultural matrix for human identity, integrated with these other aspects of culture.[12] Work is still incontrovertibly 'critical for individuals . . . a principal structure for mattering'.[13] The evidence for this is the effect on our sense of selfhood when this working culture and its practices change – which is just what has been so marked in recent decades. The focus of this discussion therefore remains specifically on changing work practices (and their implications for identity and loyalty), rather than the wider socio-economic systems in which they are embedded.

Identity and new cultures of work

Recent changes in working culture have been well documented. Casey summarizes like this. Information technology and computerization generally lead to a post-industrial economy which no longer requires as many workers. Redundancy and unemployment are more likely, and many who retain work in large organizations are reduced to insecure or short-term service activities. An automated and computer-integrated workplace combines tasks previously carried out by single-skilled workers. This requires flexibility and movement between tasks. It also blurs boundaries between old occupational specializations and the hierarchies they generated. 'Flatter' hierarchies and team work on particular projects begin to replace settled long-term structures of work. Also, with better communications, mobility and flexibility, it becomes possible and economically efficient to buy in particular skills or 'outsource' particular tasks. This means that some organizations employ only a relatively small core workforce, with other workers brought in temporarily 'like the cast and support staff of a film set in which employees are contracted for specific productions for specific time periods'.[14] There is no advantage in retaining long-term core workers for a 'down-time' of recession. Even long-term employees are frequently displaced from a settled work location by the demands, and possibilities, of globalization. In some cases there is no significant physical location to which an organization belongs. It has become largely 'virtual'.

In this situation the particular patterns of working life which could offer a settled identity are being eroded. The occupational definition of a worker (mechanic, electrician, plumber), which used to offer a recognized pathway through a whole working life, is giving way to the portfolio worker with a variety of transferable skills. The same is true in the notion of career structure. It used to be commonplace to enter a secure but potentially dynamic role within a single large organization, or related organizations. The role developed according to a recognized and mostly hierarchical structure of career phases and additional responsibilities. This generated a contract of mutual responsibilities and loyalties with the company, expressed concretely in, for example, long-term training and pension schemes. The flattening of hierarchies, establishment of teams, project-based work and general fluidity of employment largely destroy these settled structures of occupation and career. Some professions retain aspects of the older patterns, and unskilled worker have never experienced them. But their wider demise is indisputable.[15] It all amounts to what is readily described as a revolution for work relationships, and especially for the notion of contract and commitment:

> The harsh environment has caused the loss for ever of the old, long-term relational contract. This relational contract ... implied mutual commitment and trust over the long term. It was, indeed, a relationship, the severance of which was like the break-up of many relationships – sad, painful and acrimonious.[16]

The specific effects on personal identity are predictable, particularly when they are seen to operate cumulatively in the wider cultural and social context. It is fundamentally isolating and fragmenting. In 1984 this was already being described from the perspective of business analysis:

> today all the patterns are changing at once. Careers, like marriages, are more prone to abrupt endings. Work is less predictable . . . The new staging posts of life – leaving home, divorce, redundancy – do not yet have their rituals and therefore seem to each person *something that is happening to him or her alone, not part of a pattern.*[17]

More recent reflection from sociology, critical theory and political philosophy extends the analysis in a number of important ways. The demise of occupation and career means the erosion of vocation and mission which binds a life together and confers meaning to the whole narrative direction of a life. From within a career, the personal choices, relationships, and domestic changes of life outside the working environment could all derive a further framework of meaning. But without a settled and connected working life there is less continuity in roles and values to underpin these 'outside' relationships. The outcome is a 'corrosion of character'.[18] A career channelled personal aspiration into a long-term project, but without it, aspiration is easily reduced just to 'successive episodes in want satisfaction'.[19] Self-identity is also affected by the change in social recognition and solidarity. An identifiable occupation or career would be supported by union membership, class solidarity, guild affiliation or membership of a professional body. All these reinforce personal identity within webs of loyalty, allegiance and belonging. But they largely dissolve or disappear altogether in the fluid environment of knowledge-based and transferable skills and tasks.

The new form of allegiances, loyalties, and personal identity generated within working culture are scrutinized closely by Casey (a study based on North American corporate culture, but with recognizable elements in most developed post-industrial working environments).[20] It is clear that 'flatter'

systems of team work which replace rigid bureaucratic hierarchies generate considerable bonds of belonging and mission
within the team. They also provide opportunities for more
personal responsibility, initiative and autonomy, compared
to older line-management systems. This is encouraged by
corporate policy. The rhetoric of belonging and participation in corporate goals, often internalized in particular team
projects, is insistent and pervasive. The company knows it
must now 'win the socio-psychological space emptied by the
fall of unionism and occupational solidarity', especially since
the space is no longer filled by other wider narratives, whether
of nationality, religion, or science.[21] This means that a self-
conscious culture of belonging and loyalty is deliberately
cultivated. In this sense, work is being systematically intensified as a 'structure for mattering' (Handy).

The trouble is, these loyalties being generated can be
largely spurious. It is a semblance of solidarity to replace the
real solidarities of occupational, career or class belonging. It is
unreal because it is highly contingent, short-term, and subject
to all the insecurities and fluidity that the overall economic
culture imposes. In this climate the team will quickly eject its
weak links if the project is threatened – and the company does
not reciprocate the loyalty of the team by providing structured
job security, benefits and pensions. There is also a subtle
manipulation of the self which helps the company maintain
the simulation and pre-empts criticism. The older bureaucratic
and hierarchical systems, operating with ruthless instrumental reason, clearly separated values at work (efficiency,
specialization, division of labour, exclusion from overall
goals) from wider moral values in the rest of life (personal
integration, belonging, justice, love). But the new culture of
work itself uses the moral discourse of belonging and participation. It can even generate the discourse and the experience
of intimacy which is normally associated only with domestic
life or other close human relationships. In this way the separation of working values and the rest of life does not seem obvious, and the simulation it represents is masked. An individual
worker's critical capacity is easily seduced – and the collective

resistance of a union is no longer available. It produces a kind of totalitarian takeover of the worker's moral and social world which makes dissent difficult. It can invest the company with a quasi-religious authority, commanding uncritical allegiance and evangelical zeal in the employee.[22]

This is a particularly bleak analysis and Casey herself concedes it is not the whole picture. Not all is simulation. There can be real autonomy and participation within the limited parameters of a project, and that is valuable. The impetus to self-realization through flexibility, non-specialization and transferable skills, can offer genuine empowerment for the self: we are no longer defined for life by the fossilized structures of older systems. The sense of belonging, purpose, intimacy of the new working culture may be suspect and short-term but at least it can provide some significant site of relatedness. This is important when self-identity through family, religion, wider society has become precarious. It can 'shape employees . . . in a civilizing way'.[23]

Further evidence that there are more positive case studies to be found is furnished by Peter Sedgwick. There are successful small firms which emphasize independence and creativity, but which can retain a network of family and friends in their employment.[24] The tendency to totalitarianism of big corporations is resisted here. In general it is important to note the huge diversity of work experience, in which different values are operating. In some cases there are significant elements of leisure and education integrated with work, which creates new and positive possibilities of personal relatedness within the overall experience of work, and extending beyond. Identity is not always strained by work, but sometimes strengthened.[25] This returns us to the general point. Work, for better or worse, remains highly significant for our identity

Evaluating the changes

All this already implies some sort of general evaluation – and a mixed one. These changes in working practices will be viewed in much the same light as the changing dynamics of human relationships in general. A specifically Christian evaluation will do much the same. It will sift the moral complexity through the criteria of the anthropology already set out. This anthropology prizes the continuity of personhood within the processes of change, growth and self-expression. It values relationships which incorporate self-fulfilment and self-creation into a wider belonging and self-giving. Set against these goals, the ambivalence of this working culture is evident.

To the extent that it provides genuine belonging and collective purpose, and incorporates responsible, personal autonomy in the process, then it is shaping the self satisfactorily. If it is stimulating imaginative desire within an overall collective enterprise (Sedgwick's positive point about consumerism) then it is properly creative for self-identity. It fits well with an anthropology of the relational person fulfilling her identity through a purposeful narrative. It allows some sense of personal vocation within a co-operative effort of creation and production. The specific call to faithfulness will find some fertile ground to take root.

But to the extent that it is a spurious culture which manipulates the worker into this experience of co-operation – only to abandon him frequently and without ceremony – then it does immense damage to self-identity. It encourages short-term serial identities. It makes us liable to satisfy ourselves through temporary self-referential liaisons rather than a wider narrative of meaning and belonging. The element of deception is also highly damaging. The astute worker is forced into short-term collusions and role-play to succeed at work on the terms of its demands (i.e. wholesale allegiance). This compromises integrity even more acutely than the split roles generated by a more bureaucratic system – which claimed less but also deceived less. Alternatively, she becomes genuinely consumed by the allegiance, cannot sustain a joint role with life beyond work – but then finds she has sold her soul in the shifting sands of this unreliable work culture, rather than in a more worthwhile narrative. Either way, the shape of the self will lack the kind of integrity and continuity demanded by Christian anthropology.

When this experience reacts cumulatively with other fragmenting pressures of late modernity it can also deepen our more general moral and spiritual malaise. The whole narrative of our life becomes more problematic when there is no shape in any one aspect of it. When we are told that 'the issue people face today is not merely job insecurity, but more the loss of *meaning* that occurs when working life no longer has a discernible shape', we are hearing about a consequence attributed specifically to changing work practices[26] – and we are also acknowledging the wider social context which has fed it. The sense in which the *moral* malaise deepens arises because these consequences of work and wider culture do not just affect generalities of self-identity and meaning: they reinforce particular dispositions of the self, and suppress others.[27] For instance, if (as Casey says) the effect of serial work projects is to replace genuine loyalty with 'successive episodes of want satisfaction', this directly reinforces the more general destructive dispositions of 'pure' relationships. Serial want satisfaction is a dangerous flip side of Sedgwick's 'imaginative desire' when it feeds into human relationships. Similarly, if the work culture creates a disposition of 'manipulation, semblance, collusion, role play', this will undermine other close relationships under pressure. It will seed mistrust in relationships already relying heavily on risk, trust, existential commitment. It is a clear counter-culture to Christian anthropology. It subverts the call to faithfulness at almost every point.

Future developments

Given this sort of analysis it is natural to look to future changes for help. Could they reverse these trends? Probably not. Views of the future based on current tendencies do not anticipate any revival of the career or settled occupation. If anything the short-term future is likely to intensify the effect of recent developments. What has been called the 'wired' life ('fast, globally networked, project-centred') is still developing.[28] The pattern of working serially or consecutively with different projects appears to be spreading from highly trained and professional workers to other trades. The engineer who turns to business administration then consultancy is matched by the carpenter who starts a small business.

Some recent characterization of this culture, and its effects on personal identity, is even sharper than Casey's. It suggests that long-term commitment is *deliberately* rejected as an impediment to success. The commitment is not to live a particular kind of life, but to achieve particular projects. It is designed to be a life of 'discrete, even discrepant, achievements'. In practice this will mean that

> experiencing the passion involved in achieving a particular goal largely replaces the loyalty to institutions or communities . . . a project worker will commonly work with a company willing to support the project best, not remain with the one that originally inspired the project or which has employed him or her for years.[29]

This is not a life grounded in a connected narrative: it is a series of brief lives, in an almost Nietzschean sense.[30] These passionate but brief lives generate only brief habits and relationships, rather than lasting dispositions. The personal autonomy at the heart of it is expressed in the choice of free-floating values and goals rather than the personal ownership of a coherent narrative. In this characterization the engine of change is located more in the aspirations of the individual than the organizational needs of big corporations. But the totalitarian effect is the same. The demands of this 'wired life' undermine responsibilities in all other aspects of life. Loyalties to family and community which require long-term belonging are seen as 'roadblocks to personal development'. The virtues and dispositions which sustain them are neither encouraged nor honoured.[31] In such a climate faithfulness becomes all the more important in principle, but much harder in practice.

Time, place, and the possibilities of faithfulness

So how can some sort of faithfulness be re-established? The appeal for it is not new. Even before the far point of current trends became visible, a need to rehabilitate loyalty was recognized. The argument begins on the rational grounds of business efficiency. As early as 1970 Albert Hirschman argued forcefully that when customers or members of an organization deserted (or were expelled) too readily, this deprived the organization of the very voices who could best help it change.[32] In other words, loyalty could be an engine of creative change rather than a sign of stagnation. Even when 'false' loyalties created to exploit employees were unmasked, this would still motivate the worker. Moreover, the threat of loyal and creative workers to leave would motivate responsiveness in the manager. The notion of the *public* good of an organization also helps generate a creative loyalty in its members. Belief in its public value means that even if they cease to belong in one role (e.g. as employee), they know they may still need it to flourish in another role (e.g. as consumer). This is a calculating loyalty, even when the appeal is made to a public good. It is not primarily motivated by concerns for human identity. It is explicitly contrasted with 'faith' (and so faithfulness), which sometimes has to act without self-interest in view. Nonetheless, it provides at least some form of rational motivation to look further – and deeper.

What takes us further is precisely a theological and moral concern for human identity, not just the rational calculation of business efficiency. In fact these are inseparable in a working culture, so the needs of human identity must be understood whenever we attempt to reshape that culture. This is increasingly recognized, at least in general terms. For example, it has prompted a recent call for greater commitment in working culture by rehabilitating the notion of mutual contract, because 'contracts restore dignity'.[33] But what is also needed is a more specific re-evaluation of human needs based on these changes in the culture that have emerged. In particular there are the needs which arise *because of the changed role of time and place*. Both clearly matter for human identity, and both have been affected by changing working practices. As we have seen, project-based work separates time into discrete bundles. Workers are also physically displaced by the need for flexibility, mobility and the opportunities of communication and information technology. This is a core factor in its effect on personal identity. It certainly makes any kind of faithfulness problematic. Faithfulness requires connected time and a settled place to facilitate these temporal connections. So this focuses the need. Any call to faithfulness within the current working culture will have to address this. It must find ways of securing a connected narrative for workers through the disconnections they are experiencing. That is how it will make faithfulness more possible.

The indirect expression of obligation, i.e. 'to make faithfulness more possible', is a good way of articulating the moral and social obligations of an institution or corporate body. This is because the attempt to specify moral obligation directly in a corporate context is not straightforward, and simply to call a company to 'faithfulness' is unrealistic. It is asking an impersonal organization to fulfil an essentially personal moral concept. This makes sense only analogously. There are personal dimensions to the action of a corporate body, but it is still structured by an organizing constitution which may facilitate personal life but cannot *be* wholly personal. Nor can it be wholly moral: as Reinhold Niebuhr has pointed out, a corporate body is always constrained in its moral action when compared to an individual agent, simply by virtue of being corporate.[34]

At the same time, corporate bodies are called to moral account in some way. In Christian terms there is clear teaching that both the state and the Church are subject to God's judgement or approval. In secular terms there is the acknowledged field of business ethics. This is growing rapidly. To demonstrate ethical accountability to shareholders, customers, stakeholders and the wider society is increasingly part of an organization's remit and reputation.[35] It also means extending notions of corporate responsibility to staff and employees beyond the minimum statutory requirements of employment law. This 'ethical' reputation may still be linked with successful commercial performance, but its meaning cannot be reduced to it. It certainly carries a company beyond a single-minded pursuit of maximum profitability.[36] Rendering a moral account in some way is therefore part of current corporate discourse – and an aim of providing the conditions in which something like faithfulness is made more possible should not be out of place. It is a possible way of rendering that moral account. As the state is called to secure peace and justice to make 'a godly life' possible, so a company can be called upon to provide conditions in which faithfulness is more possible. This is not unrealistic. A company has complex and sometimes conflicting roles and responsibilities, in relation to employees, customers, shareholders and the wider society: an obligation of facilitating loyalty is a co-ordinating notion which can make moral and practical sense in all these roles.

What might this mean in practice? We need to return to this question of time. A company must help its employees to make connections through time. An overall presumption of facilitating faithfulness will push the company to provide an overall narrative of meaning at work, rather than discrete bundles of meaning. This means there must be some effort to create connections between projects, both within a single company and for new workers or consultants brought into a company from outside. The connection need not be only through the 'product' of the project. It can be through a transmitted recognition of the knowledge and skills (and personality) brought to the project by the worker.[37] Because the knowledge and skills are no longer rooted in a settled career structure or socially recognized occupation, they have been separated from the person as he moves on from project to project. But they still constitute a constellation of aptitudes and attitudes which help express his identity, and this needs to be recognized and transmitted in the move to another project or company. An employer's reference or particular sets of training qualifications are only the beginning. What is required are new forms of corporate and social recognition. This may have to begin with new educational and vocational priorities which will offer an initial recognized qualification for wired life.[38] Still more will be needed for long-term social identity. Unions, guild affiliations and professional bodies are all models which have operated effectively in this way in a different working culture. Now there will need to be a quasi-professional body which recognizes workers and consultants with largely fluid, knowledge-based skills. Belonging to such a body can help hold even the transient project worker within a wider narrative of meaning. It can connect her working life through time, even when the product or company itself is constantly changing. A more modest aspiration, but equally important, will be a policy to strengthen working relationships through time within the company. As long as it remains possible in a dynamic context, structural stability of working relationships must be better established. Unnecessary rotation of staff must be avoided. The benefits of providing this possibility for 'faithful' working relationships will be evident, the dangers of failing to provide it all too apparent in some high profile corporate disasters.[39]

The presumption of facilitating faithfulness will also push companies to provide a connected narrative between work and wider life. This can be achieved through the product itself. A deliberate attempt to demonstrate the value of the product in society connects the worker with a continuous thread of meaning when the particular project is long finished. This is easy to demonstrate if the project is building a bridge or raising money for hospital equipment. It is less obvious when the effort is being poured into luxury consumer products, or the making of money in financial markets. But it is usually possible to make some connections with wider social value and meaning, and these connections must be deliberately brought into the culture of the workplace. It is implicit in what Hirschman briefly alludes to as the 'public good' of work – but it needs to be made explicit.[40] The presumption also needs to be worked out in the wider world of the worker herself, not just the product. The worker's other roles with family and home community must be recognized.[41] The project team and the short-term passion of the project itself must not be allowed to supplant these other relationships. Flexible working hours and *place* of work can provide more access to family and home community. More positively, a company can recognize this wider world by sponsoring its local education, nursery groups, voluntary activities. This culture of connections prevents the totalitarian tendencies of working culture. It enhances and connects the overall identity of the worker in a wider world of meaning which persists even when a particular work project has been short term. The possibility and importance of making these wider connections has long been recognized. A case study of Levi Strauss & Co notes that 'the company has always encouraged its employees to get involved with the local community', and cites initiatives taken as long ago as 1968, as well as more recent developments.[42] It is all the more needed now to counter the effects of the 'wired' working life – which abstracts the worker's wider identity from the community and then spits it out altogether.

Similar presumptions must also apply to the individual worker herself. Here again there is an important qualification. Faithfulness to an institution or a job is a relationship to something with impersonal elements. So the dynamics of the relationship cannot exactly mirror faithfulness in interpersonal relationships. For instance, when the job ceases, and if there are no continuing benefits from the institution itself, it is hard to see any residual meaning to faithfulness which the worker has to carry forward. He cannot continue to express loyalty to the job itself (though he may continue personal loyalty to people associated with it). Nonetheless, just as corporate bodies are still held to moral account in some way, so too is the individual member or worker. Generally speaking there is still some moral meaning or obligation in relation to a job. Not least, there is the tradition of personal *vocation* to work which has already been established. It is an integral part of human identity. In Christian terms, productive work is a co-operative endeavour with the Creator himself. A job and the institution which structures it therefore deserves at least an analogy of faithfulness from the worker. This will seem more compelling when the job or project is chosen and the productive enterprise is morally fitting. But even in the more usual situation where workers have less choice and the 'product' has no obvious moral attraction, some presumptions of faithfulness still operate. Just as inherited kinship relationships still require faithful behaviour in the fulfilment of our identity, so too does the work of a given job.

How will this presumption of faithfulness work in practice for the employee? The key lies again in the connections that have to be made through time – between projects within work, and between work and wider life. It is when the individual pursues both these connections that he best fulfils his relationship with a project or company. Within work this may mean opting for related projects, wherever choice is possible. It means a presumption to stay within a field of endeavour, if not a single company, whenever the opportunity presents itself. Because the dynamics of faithfulness include willingness to change, this is not a roadblock to creativity and flexibility. It entails a responsibility to the company (and to oneself) to retrain and renew creativity and energy. But this is still sought within the overall continuities of a job, rather than by deliberate discontinuity. Within wider life, it means making the attempt to use the product or the skills of work in relation to the wider community. When a small business contributes to the local economy this should be part of the perceived purpose of the business rather than a disconnected by-product. In the same way, when the worker brings her own skills from the workplace into a voluntary organization this should be seen as a natural extension of her working identity into a wider identity, not a conflicting loyalty. Again, this helps bind the identity of the worker to a wider narrative of time (and place) which will persist even when the job ends.

The economic and social realism of this sort of disposition is open to question. But there is some evidence that it can develop, even within the overall fluidity and competitiveness demanded in current working life. It is described as a new kind of entrepreneurism.[43] The impetus for it comes in the drive to improve and achieve, and incorporates significant elements of self-expression and self-creation. But the object of the endeavour is less focused on an 'abstracted' target set by the company, or oneself. It is directed to the improvement of the whole community of the company itself, or the wider social or community context of a project. It is a socially embedded enterprise, driven by a desire to relate the purposes of the work beyond itself. Some of the characteristics of career re-emerge in this sort of working culture. The continuous commitment to the social relations of work establishes a socially recognized identity for the worker and an overall narrative framework for him to give shape to his working life. But because this framework may have to span different projects, it does not depend on reinstating the more rigid structures of traditional careers and occupations.

A prophetic postscript?

One other question is always raised by this sort of discussion. Is it sufficiently radical? A Christian critique of current working practices may well begin by encouraging this sort of transformation within the existing economic and social conditions that help shape those practices. It may even look for some positive elements within those wider conditions, as Peter Sedgwick is willing to do. But should it also press for more radical changes in the social and economic system itself, as other commentators insist?[44] This is a question that must be registered, even if a serious answer lies beyond the scope of this book. Yet whatever answer is given, this much at least should now be clear. What matters most is to ensure that any call to change recognizes what is happening to *people*. The effects of working culture on self-identity are profound. Some of them are currently disastrous. If these effects cannot be addressed by reform from within, then we may have to listen to those more radical prophets. But either way, this must be for the sake of people, not just the economy, nor even ideology.

CONCLUSION

TIME, CHANGE, IDENTITY: THE CALL TO FAITHFULNESS

When Edward Thomas described a glimpse of England in the brief pause of a passing train he wrote only a few taut lines. But they touch on universal experience. They express both the pain and the possibility of existence.

> And for that minute a blackbird sang
> Close by, and round him, mistier,
> Farther and farther, all the birds
> Of Oxfordshire and Gloucestershire. (from 'Adlestrop')[1]

The pain is in the inexorable passing of the moment. The train drew up there temporarily, 'unwontedly'. It would move on. The possibility lies in the memory of the moment with its strange capacity to universalize the particular. Both time and space are expanded. The single birdsong conveys *all* birdsong; 'the glimpsed good place is made permanent' (R. S. Thomas). In some way neither time or place are lost but taken up in something transcendent. The very particularity of the moment and the place is the route to its universality, perhaps the only route. The image of a train conveys this. The 'permanence' of the moment can only be secured because the train moves on. It is in this curious connection between transience and permanence that pain and possibility are reconciled, a philosophical conundrum is resolved, and a moment of eternity is secured – in the experience of the traveller.

But what manner of moving on is it? A simple change of time and place is not enough in itself. Change in itself is not saving, merely inevitable. It must carry something with it. It must carry with it whatever is good from the past, for the future, and even from the future. Better still, *we* must carry this with *us*. That is how we shall include permanence in our passing. Thomas's traveller expresses this by being a traveller, a continuous subject of connected experiences, holding them in his own narrative. The intensity of the particular moment recorded depends on that, and carries all that.

The plea of this book is to negotiate change in just this way. We maintain and fulfil our identity, and the identity of others, by carrying the moments of our existence, roles and relationships with us *through* time. We cannot hold on to them by freezing a particular moment of time. But nor should we try to sever ourselves from them as time moves on: we must stay with them through time. The worst of our moments need time and change to be redeemed. The best are kept through time by growth, not possession. This is as true for the ordinary stuff and structures of our lives as it is for rarer moments of religious or imaginative intensity. It needs to be tried in domestic relationships and working practices, just as much as in prayer and poetry. It is the way of faithfulness.

This pattern is rooted in God. God's being is dynamic, but he/she does not lose any part of it within that dynamism. God holds his own experience of change within his own being. This helps define God's identity. In this way God is both responsive and essentially unchanging. God's relationship with his creation is the direct expression of this identity. He does not sever himself from any part of his creation, but responds to its own changes. Whatever the changes and loss of our temporal experience, God carries them too within his own relationship with us, and redeems them. God *is* faithful.

A call to faithfulness follows for us. I believe it is a universal call. It will fulfil human identity and the human condition as such. We all need to be faithful in all ways possible in our fallen and finite condition. There is no reason to be sceptical about the universal status of this belief. I repeat here what the introduction set out. *Pace* postmodernism, at least some anthropological, theological and moral presumptions can be held for all. There is no a priori reason to think universal beliefs are necessarily unreasonable, unworkable, or oppressive. They become so only if they are abstracted from practices and imposed in arbitrary rules, regardless of social context; or if they are expressed too idealistically (like Royce's principle of 'loyalty to loyalty'). By contrast, a mature notion of faithfulness is quite different. It is not a timeless rule. It can be traced through a variety of intellectual and social contexts as a continuous but creative thread of *character*. In this way it accommodates change at the same time as it sustains a connected identity through change.

This claim to universality makes it a public plea from a public theology. That does not make it any easier to put into practice. In a complex and fast-changing world any disposition of character is difficult to form and perplexing to live out. Even in a relatively stable world there will be enough setback and disappointment to test and create the meaning of faithful character. As Royce said, 'strain, endurance, sacrifice, toil . . . teach us what loyalty is'. But although it makes it no easier, its universality does motivate us to try. It strengthens our nerve against the creeping moral paralysis that change and complexity produces. It invites us to find common ground with other moral, religious and political traditions which prize fidelity. Like other icons, it provides a definite moral shape to aspire to and live within – and commend to others. We shall fail and need grace and forgiveness, of course. But we can try.

Because the heart of this faithfulness lies in the identity of God, we may even expect to see some fruits of the endeavour. Its empirical success will not be obvious or short term. But we will still find it works. It will make satisfying moral life more possible, not just for ourselves, but for others, and for society generally. As Joe's faithfulness to Pip in *Great Expectations* helped create Pip's character, so will any attempt to be faithful. We may even find it brings joy. Why not? There is a connection between faithfulness and joy in the way we are made. We have it on good authority: *'Well done thou good and faithful servant, enter into the joy of your master.'*

The peculiar urgency of it now is evident. It is badly needed to bind the fragments of the selves that are still breaking up two decades after Kundera's memorable warning. Without fidelity we splinter into a thousand fragments. But with fidelity, by the grace of God, who knows what can be healed?

NOTES

Introduction: Identity, change and faithfulness: a theological task

1 Francis Thompson, *The Hound of Heaven*.
2 Cf. A. C. Thiselton, *Interpreting God and the Postmodern Self* (Grand Rapids: Eerdmans, 1995), p. 121.
3 Frank Kermode, 'Waiting for the End' in Malcolm Bull (ed.), *Apocalypse Theory and the End of the World* (Oxford: Blackwell, 1995).
4 See for example D. W. Hardy, *God's Ways with the World* (Edinburgh: T&T Clark, 1996).
5 Rowan Williams, *Lost Icons* (T&T Clark, Edinburgh, 2000).

1 Faithfulness and loyalty: some recent compass points

1 Josiah Royce, *The Philosophy of Loyalty* (New York: Macmillan, 1908). References from John J. McDermott (ed.), *The Basic Writings of Josiah Royce*, Vol. 2 (Chicago: University of Chicago, 1969).
2 Josiah Royce, *The Problem of Christianity* II (New York: Macmillan, 1913), p. 81.
3 *Philosophy of Loyalty*, p. 910.
4 *Philosophy of Loyalty*, p. 993.
5 *Philosophy of Loyalty*, pp. 997, 1005.
6 *Philosophy of Loyalty*, p. 863.
7 *Philosophy of Loyalty*, p. 922.
8 *Philosophy of Loyalty*, p. 894.
9 *Philosophy of Loyalty*, p. 943.
10 *Philosophy of Loyalty*, p. 907.
11 Cf. Josiah Royce, *Race Questions, Provincialism and Other*

American Problems (New York: Macmillan, 1908). There is a
wide range of contemporary support for this from a variety of
political, social, philosophical commentators, by no means all
of whom would call themselves communitarian: cf. Alasdair
MacIntyre, *After Virtue* (London: Duckworth, 1981); John
Gray, *Beyond the New Right* (London: Routledge, 1993);
Stephen Clark, *Civil Peace and Sacred Order* (Oxford: Clarendon
Press, 1989).

12 *Philosophy of Loyalty*, p. 973.

13 *Philosophy of Loyalty*, p. 971.

14 Cf. *Race Questions*, e.g. p. 101.

15 J. J. McDermott, in his introduction to *The Philosophy of Loyalty*
(Nashville: Vanderbilt University Press, 1995).

16 See for example Peter Fuss, *The Moral Philosophy of Josiah Royce*
(Cambridge, Mass.: Harvard University Press, 1965).

17 Gabriel Marcel, *Being and Having* (ET Westminster: Dacre
Press, 1949), p. 41. See also Gabriel Marcel, *The Existential
Background of Human Dignity* (ET Cambridge, Mass.: Harvard
University Press, 1963).

18 *Being and Having*, pp. 45, 46.

19 *Being and Having*, p. 54.

20 H. R. Niebuhr, *Radical Monotheism and Western Culture*
(London: Faber & Faber, 1961). Cf. also his *The Responsible Self*
(New York: Harper & Row, 1963).

21 *Radical Monotheism and Western Culture*, pp. 33–4.

22 *Radical Monotheism and Western Culture*, p. 18.

23 *Radical Monotheism and Western Culture*, p. 47.

24 See for example Paul Ramsey, *The Patient as Person* (New
Haven: Yale University Press, 1970), which applies the 'canon
of loyalty' to medical ethics. Cf. also Joseph Allen, *Love
and Conflict: a covenantal model of Christian ethics* (Nashville:
Abingdon Press, 1984); also Margaret Farley, *Personal Commitments* (San Francisco: Harper & Row, 1990).

25 J. J. McDermott, in *The Philosophy of Loyalty*, p. xix.

2 Divine identity

1 Cf. Colin Gunton, *The One, the Three and the Many* (Cambridge:
Cambridge University Press, 1993).

2 This is the central argument of an earlier book. See Vernon

White, *Atonement and Incarnation: an essay in universalism and particularity* (Cambridge: Cambridge University Press, 1991).

3 See Nicholas Wolterstorff, 'Is it possible and desirable for theologians to recover from Kant?', *Modern Theology* 14, no. 1, January 1998.

4 As Pannenberg insists, there is a metaphysical claim in the insistence that God is one which is intrinsic to the meaning of God's identity over against all other gods. Cf. Wolfhart Pannenberg, *Systematic Theology* Vol 1 (ET Edinburgh: T&T Clark, 1991), pp. 67ff.

5 Thus Paul Ricoeur. When he analyses human personal identity through the structures of story-telling, the fundamental datum of enduring personal reality is described as self-hood: 'even with . . . the loss of sameness-identity of the hero, we do not escape the problematic of selfhood'. Paul Ricoeur, *Oneself as Another* (ET Chicago: University of Chicago Press, 1992), p. 196.

6 See pp. 46–55 below.

7 See R. H. King, *The Meaning of God* (London: SCM, 1974), p. 48. In this respect he follows Stuart Hampshire.

8 Cf. Vernon White, *The Fall of a Sparrow: a concept of special divine action* (Exeter: Paternoster, 1985).

9 The literature is immense and growing. Keith Ward, *Divine Action* (London: Collins, 1990) reviews much of it.

10 See for example Vincent Brummer, *The Model of Love* (Cambridge: Cambridge University Press, 1993).

3 *Divine faithfulness*

1 N. H. Snaith, *The Distinctive Ideas of the Old Testament* (London: Epworth Press, 1944), p. 99.

2 *New International Dictionary of Old Testament Theology and Exegesis*, Vol. 2 (Carlisle: Paternoster, 1997), p. 214.

3 See for example Allen, *Love and Conflict*. He distinguishes two major types of biblical covenant: the 'promising covenant' (with Noah, Abraham, David) where the main emphasis is on divine promising, and the 'law covenant' where more emphasis is placed on mutual obligation.

4 G. von Rad, *Old Testament Theology* II (ET London: SCM, 1965), p. 371.

5 cf. Walter Brueggemann, *Theology of the Old Testament* (Minneapolis: Fortress Press, 1997). Israel's 'focus on fidelity' (p. 226) proves itself in the face of Yahweh's apparent unreliability and hiddenness.

6 Pannenberg, *Systematic Theology*, p. 160 (emphasis mine).

7 E. W. Nicholson, *God and His People: covenant and theology in the Old Testament* (Oxford: Oxford University Press, 1986), p. 216 (emphasis mine).

8 Hebrews 6.17.

9 Cf. Nicholas Sagovsky, *Ecumenism, Christian Origins and the Practice of Communion* (Cambridge: Cambridge University Press, 2000): 'Christ *is* the covenant.'

10 Cf. Vernon White, *Atonement and Incarnation*.

11 Thus the Johannine teaching about the Spirit follows the Last Supper, the sign of the new covenant. The Kingdom is associated with the covenant in the echoes of such phrases as the *establishing* of a Kingdom, just as a covenant is *established*. (e.g. Luke 22.29).

12 D. Ritschl, *The Christian Doctrine of Justification and Reconciliation* (Edinburgh: T&T Clark, 1871), 1:1, cited in Alister McGrath, *Iustitia Dei* (Cambridge: Cambridge University Press, 1986), Vol. 2, p. 162; cf. also P. Collinson, 'The late medieval Church and its reformation (1400–1600)' in J. McManners, *The Oxford Illustrated History of Christianity* (Oxford: Oxford University Press, 1990), pp. 258–9. The ascription 'canon within the canon' is by Ernest Kasemann.

13 See especially J. D. G. Dunn's discussion in *The Theology of Paul the Apostle* (Edinburgh: T&T Clark, 1998), pp. 335–42.

14 Catherine Keller, 'The theology of Moltmann, feminism, and the future', in Miroslav Volf, Carmen Krieg, Thomas Kucharz (eds), *The Future of Theology* (Grand Rapids: Eerdmans, 1996).

15 Cf. Richard Bauckham (ed.), *God Will be All in All: the eschatology of Jürgen Moltmann* (Edinburgh: T&T Clark, 1999), e.g. pp. 35–41, Jürgen Moltmann, 'The World in God or God in the World'.

16 See for example Paul Helm (ed.), *Jonathan Edwards. Treatise on Grace* (Cambridge : James Clarke, 1971).

17 Aquinas, *Summa Theologiae*, Vol. 2, 1a,9,2 (ET London: Eyre & Spottiswoode, 1964), p.129.

18 *Summa*, 1a,9,2.

19 *Summa*, 1,8,1.

20 Thomas Weinandy, *Does God Suffer?* (T&T Clark, Edinburgh, 2000), pp.135–6.

21 *Does God Suffer?* pp.135–6.

22 Karl Barth, *Church Dogmatics* II:1, Ch. 6:31:2 (ET Edinburgh: T&T Clark, 1957).

23 *Church Dogmatics* II:1, pp. 491–2.

24 *Church Dogmatics* II:1, p. 502.

25 *Church Dogmatics* II:1, p. 494.

26 *Church Dogmatics* II:1, p. 495.

27 Cf. Gijsbert van den Brink, 'Capable of anything? The omnipotence of God', in van den Brink and Marcel Sarot (eds), *Understanding the Attributes of God* (ET New York: Peter Lang, 1999).

28 Pannenberg, *Systematic Theology*, p. 436.

29 *Systematic Theology*, p. 438.

30 *Systematic Theology*, p. 438.

31 *Does God Suffer?* p. 62.

32 *Does God Suffer?* p. 136, n. 69. Weinandy proposes a sort of modified Cambridge change, which is not without its own problems.

33 See Vernon White, 'The future of theology', in M. Percy (ed.), *Calling Time* (Sheffield: Sheffield Academic Press, 2000).

34 Frances Young, *Face to Face: a narrative essay in the theology of suffering* (Edinburgh: T&T Clark, 1990).

35 Cf. Colin Gunton's early discussion comparing Barth and Process Theology in *Becoming and Being: the doctrine of God in Charles Hartshorne and Karl Barth* (Oxford: Oxford University Press, 1978).

36 Cf. Denys Turner, *The Darkness of God: negativity in Christian mysticism* (Cambridge: Cambridge University Press, 1995).

37 Cf. Vernon White, 'Re-enchanting the world: a fresh look at the God of mystical theology', in *Theology*, Vol. CIII, no. 815 (2000).

38 Pannenberg, *Systematic Theology*, p. 71 (emphasis mine).

39 W. H. Vanstone, *Love's Endeavour, Love's Expense* (London: DLT, 1977); cf. my discussion in *The Fall of a Sparrow*, pp. 87ff.

40 Joseph Fletcher, *Situation Ethics* (London: SCM, 1966).
41 See further below, p. 67.

4 *Human identity*

1 Cf. Harriet Harris, 'Should we say that personhood is relational?', in *The Scottish Journal of Theology* 51.2 (Edinburgh: T&T Clark, 1998).
2 Alistair I. McFadyen, *The Call to Personhood. A Christian theory of the individual in social relations* (Cambridge: Cambridge University Press, 1990), p. 93.
3 For a fuller discussion, see *Paying Attention to People*, p.184.
4 Cf. Stanley Rudman, *Concepts of Person* (Cambridge: Cambridge University Press, 1997), p. 178.
5 Most of what follows in the ensuing paragraphs about personhood and relationality summarizes what I have argued at greater length in *Paying Attention to People. An essay on individualism and Christian belief* (especially ch. 4).
6 Both Ian Ramsey's seminal work, *Religious Language. An empirical placing of theological phrases* (London: SCM, 1957) which engages specifically with empiricism, and the apophatic way of the via negativa, contribute to this process of meaning through qualification. Both do so in an enduring way which still gives possibilities to theological language, even in a postmodern context. Cf. A. C. Thiselton's use of Ramsey in *Interpreting God and the Postmodern Self*.
7 Derek Parfit, *Reasons and Persons* (Oxford: Clarendon Press, 1984).
8 Paul Ricoeur, *Oneself as Another*, p. 196.
9 Cf. David Cecil's comments in e.g. *Early Victorian Novelists*.
10 It is not just a recent interest, of course. Karl Marx, amongst other figures from the past, should not be forgotten: 'Man is ... a *zoon politikon*, not only a social animal, but an animal which can develop into an individual only in society.' *A Contribution to the Critique of Political Economy* 1857 (ET Chicago, 1913).
11 See especially John Zizioulas, *Being as Communion. Studies in personhood and the Church* (London: DLT, 1985) and Alan Torrance, *Persons in Communion. Trinitarian description and human participation* (Edinburgh: T&T Clark, 1996).

12 Ricoeur, *Oneself as Another*.

13 See especially Colin Gunton, *The One, the Three and the Many*.

14 See Vernon White, *Atonement and Incarnation*, where this is more fully argued.

15 Wisdom literature of the Old Testament might be considered an exception. But this does not claim constitutive or saving status for human identity in the same way that major biblical narratives or doctrines of God have done.

16 See Alasdair MacIntyre, *After Virtue* (London: Duckworth, 2nd edition 1990); *Whose Justice? Which Rationality?* (London: Duckworth, 1988); 'A partial response to my critics' in J. Horton and S. Mendus (eds), *After MacIntyre* (Oxford: Polity Press, 1994).

17 See for example A. Nygren, *Agape and Eros* (ET London: SPCK, 1932); D. D. Williams, *The Spirit and the Forms of Love* (Welwyn: Nisbet, 1968); Oliver O'Donovan, *The Problem of Self-Love in St. Augustine* (New Haven: Yale University Press, 1980); Vincent Brummer, *The Model of Love*. See also Vernon White, *Paying Attention to People*, Ch. 9.

18 Ricoeur, *Oneself as Another*, Studies 7–9. Cf. David Ford's helpful discussion in *Self and Salvation* (Cambridge: Cambridge University Press, 1999), pp. 90–4.

5 *The call to human faithfulness*

1 Cf. Allen, *Love and Conflict*, pp. 44, 45: '[All] kinds of covenants require faithfulness . . . though what constitutes faithfulness depends in some respects upon the kind of covenant . . . Faithfulness of an appropriate kind is properly a requirement of every [covenantal] human relationship.'

2 Colossians 1.22–23.

3 John 15.12.

4 Matthew 5.6.

5 1 Corinthians 13.7.

6 B. W. Anderson, 'Covenant', in Bruce M. Metzger and Michael D. Coogan (eds), *The Oxford Companion to the Bible* (Oxford: Oxford University Press, 1993).

7 Genesis 2.24; Mark 10.8–9.

8 Ephesians 5.28.

9 Cf. Deuteronomy 13.6–11.

10 Luke 8.21 and Mark 10.29.

11 Cf. Stephen Barton's discussion, *Life Together* (Edinburgh: T&T Clark, 2001), pp. 47–9.

12 See Charles Taylor, *Sources of the Self* (Cambridge: Cambridge University Press, 1989), pp. 215ff.

13 E.g. 1 Kings 14.16.

14 E.g. Jeremiah 8.

15 2 Samuel 7.19.

16 2 Corinthians 16.

17 Ephesians 1.24.

18 Mark 12.17.

19 1 Timothy 2.1–2.

20 Barth, *Church Dogmatics* II:2, p. 524 (emphasis mine). Cf. Michael Banner, *Christian Ethics and Contemporary Moral Problems* (Cambridge: Cambridge University Press, 1999), Ch.1.

21 Cf. Stanley Rudman: 'if we examine what is happening in social theory and in philosophical ethics, we find signs of a converging trend to give more weight to tradition and community in ethics, . . . this corresponds with our understanding of persons in relation and with the ethical insights of Christian faith' (*Concepts of Person and Christian Ethics*, p. 229).

22 See especially Jean Porter, *The Recovery of Virtue* (London: SPCK, 1994), in conversation with MacIntyre.

23 See especially Stanley Hauerwas, *A Community of Character* (Notre Dame, Ind.: University of Notre Dame, 1981); *The Peaceable Kingdom* (London: SCM, 1984); see also *Truthfulness and Tragedy* (Notre Dame, Ind.: University of Notre Dame, 1977).

24 See especially *Truthfulness and Tragedy*.

25 For a judicious and valuable discussion see for example John Thomson, 'The Ecclesiology of Stanley Hauerwas' (unpublished doctoral thesis, University of Nottingham 2001).

6 A contemporary context: change, identity and the problem of time

1 Milan Kundera, *The Unbearable Lightness of Being* (London: Faber and Faber, 1984); Simone Weil, *The Need for Roots* (London: Ark, 1987).

2 Martin Heidegger, *Being and Time* (ET Oxford: Blackwell, 1973).

3 A valuable recent survey, particularly in relation to literature, is Paul Fiddes, *The Promised End. Eschatology in theology and literature* (Oxford: Blackwell, 2000).

4 I am indebted to Paul Fiddes for some of these insights into Eliot. Fiddes, *The Promised End*, Ch. 5, 'The eternal moment'.

5 Ricoeur, *Time and Narrative*.

6 See especially Don Cupitt, *The Time Being* (London: SCM, 1992).

7 See for example Brian Hebblethwaite, *The Ocean of Truth. A defence of objective theism* (Cambridge: Cambridge University Press, 1988); Stephen White, *Don Cupitt and the Future of Doctrine* (London: SCM, 1994) and A. C. Thiselton, *Interpreting God and the Postmodern Self* (Pt III).

8 See Fiddes, *The Promised End*, pp. 135–8.

9 Ricoeur, *Time and Narrative*, Vol. 1, pp. 26ff.

10 See especially Barth's *Epistle to the Romans* (ET Oxford: Oxford University Press, 1933).

11 Jürgen Moltmann, *The Way of Jesus Christ. Christology in messianic dimensions* (ET London: SCM, 1990), p. 303.

12 The is the major concern of his earlier book ,*Theology of Hope* (ET London: SCM, 1967).

13 See for example Moltmann, *The Trinity and the Kingdom of God.. The doctrine of God* (ET London: SCM, 1981); *The Spirit of Life. A Universal Affirmation* (ET London: SCM, 1992).

14 See especially Wolfhart Pannenberg, *Jesus – God and Man* (ET London: SCM, 1968).

15 By this process events do not just change meaning, they change in being. See Pannenberg, *Metaphysics and the Idea of God* (ET Edinburgh: T&T Clark, 1990), pp. 95–104.

16 See especially Pannenberg, *Basic Questions in Theology* (ET London: SCM, 1970–73), esp. Vol. 2.

17 Some critics find Pannenberg's sense of completion in this future an unacceptable 'closure' in principle, whatever openness remains in our perception of it in practice. See Fiddes, *The Promised End*

18 Ford, *Self and Salvation*, esp. pp. 152–62.

19 *Self and Salvation*, p. 154–5.

20 *Self and Salvation*, p. 162.

21 See Thiselton, *Interpreting God and the Postmodern Self* (esp. Pt IV) for documentation of this debate.

22 Hans-George Gadamer, *Truth and Method* (ET London: Sheed & Ward, 1993).

23 See Vernon White, *The Fall of a Sparrow*, and *Atonement and Incarnation*.

24 Ford, *Self and Salvation*.

7 *Limits and possibilities*

1 See for example Ford, *Self and Salvation* – though he does not apply this specifically to the notion of faithfulness.

2 Cf. Hauerwas, *Truthfulness and Tragedy*.

3 Margaret A. Farley, *Personal Commitments*.

4 *Personal Commitments*, pp. 57–8.

5 This is the view of José Ortega y Gasset, *On Love. Aspects of a single theme* (London: Gollancz, 1959).

6 Vincent Brummer, *The Model of Love*, p. 172.

7 Margaret Farley, *Personal Commitments*, pp. 74ff.

8 William Schweiker, *Responsibility and Christian Ethics* (Cambridge: Cambridge University Press, 1995), pp. 167–8.

9 Schweiker, *Responsibility and Christian Ethics*, Ch. 4.

10 The move to sheer relationality is set up by John Milbank, *Theology and Social Theory* (Oxford: Blackwell, 1990) – but strongly resisted by e.g. Colin Gunton, *The One, the Three, and the Many*.

11 But as noted before, this is a contested thesis. See n. 11, p. 52 above.

12 MacIntyre, *After Virtue*, p. 172.

13 See especially J-F. Lyotard, *The Postmodern Condition: A Report on Knowledge* (ET Manchester: Manchester University Press, 1992).

14 For a useful summary of some of these issues and their inter-connectedness, see J. D. G. Dunn, *The Theology of Paul the Apostle*.

8 *Practices in personal relationships*

1 Cf. Edward Shils, *Tradition* (London: Faber, 1981).

2 See Anthony Giddens, *The Consequences of Modernity* (Cambridge: Polity Press, 1990).

3 See Anthony Giddens, *Modernity and Self-Identity* (Cambridge: Polity Press, 1991).

4 For specific studies on family life cf. A. H. Halsey, 'Foreword' in Norman Dennis and George Erdos, *Families without Fatherhood* (London: IEA Health and Welfare Unit, 1993); Patricia Morgan, *Farewell to the Family? Public policy and family breakdown in Britain and the USA* (London: IEA Health and Welfare Unit, 1995). Research cited in Adrian Thatcher, *Marriage After Modernity* (Sheffield: Sheffield Academic Press, 1999). But see also Joseph Rowntree Foundation Report 1997, cited in support of the contrary view, maintaining poverty as the main source of damage to children (Suzanne Moore, *Independent* 24.6.98). For more general studies on individualism and commitment see for example Robert N. Bellah, *Habits of the Heart: Individualism and Commitment in American Life* (Berkeley: University of California Press, 1985); cf. also Margaret Farley, *Personal Commitments*, Ch 1.

5 See Don Browning, 'World family trends' in Robin Gill (ed.), *The Cambridge Companion to Christian Ethics* (Cambridge: Cambridge University Press, 2001). He cites summaries of evolutionary theory on family formation and 'kin altruism' in e.g. P. van der Berghe, *Human Family Systems: An Evolutionary View* (New York: Elsevier, 1979); M. Daly and M. Wilson, *Sex, Evolution, and Behaviour* (Belmont: Wadsworth, 1983).

6 Cf. John Snarey, *How Fathers Care for the Next Generation: a four decade study* (Cambridge, Mass.: Harvard University Press, 1993); David Popenoe, 'The evolution of marriage and the problem of stepfamilies: a biosocial perspective', in Alan Booth and Judy Dunn (eds), *Stepfamilies: Who Benefits? Who Does Not?* (Hillsdale: Erlbaum, 1994). Research cited in Browning, 'World family trends'. Evidence is also accumulated in Adrian Thatcher, *Marriage After Modernity* (Sheffield: Sheffield Academic Press, 1999), Ch. 5.

7 Browning, 'World family trends', p. 246.

8 In the Gospel narratives where Jesus welcomes children his primary concern seems to be to establish value for the *subordinate social role* that children and servants exemplified: see for example Mark 9.33–37.

9 Ephesians 6.4.

10 Augustine, *On the Good of Marriage*.

11 Thatcher, *Marriage After Modernity*.

12 Cf. Susan Moller Okin, *Justice, Gender and the Family* (New York: Basic Books, 1989).

13 E.g. Galatians 3.28.

14 Lisa Sowle Cahill, *Sex, Gender and Christian Ethics* (Cambridge: Cambridge University Press, 1996), p. 107, quoted in Thatcher, *Marriage After Modernity*, p.160.

15 *Something to Celebrate. Valuing families in Church and society* (London: Church House Publishing, 1995). One example of its real engagement with current social realities is its discussion of cohabitation. On the one hand it evaluates the practice as falling short of the full commitment which stable family relationships require, liable to damaging insecurities. But it also acknowledges and affirms it as a possible 'stage on the way' to full commitment.

16 Therapy is not a single authority but a cluster of different schools with a variety of effects. Giddens's own assessment of therapy is properly nuanced to take account of this. See for example *Modernity and Self-Identity*, pp. 179–80.

17 See Christopher Lasch, *The Culture of Narcissism: American life in an age of diminishing expectations* (New York: Norton, 1978).

18 Giddens has some criticisms of Lasch. See Giddens, *Modernity and Self Identity*, pp.171–4.

19 Giddens, *Modernity and Self-Identity*, p. 177, citing Judith Stacey, *Brave New Families* (New York: Basic Books, 1990); emphasis mine.

20 *Ageing. A Report from the Church of England Board of Social Responsibility* (London: Church House Publishing, 1990), p. 86.

21 See for example David Parker, 'The early traditions of Jesus' saying on divorce', *Theology* 96.773 (1993), cited in Thatcher, *Marriage After Modernity*, pp. 256–7.

22 Ephesians 5.28.

23 1 Corinthians 13.4–7.

24 See for instance Oliver O'Donovan, *The Problem of Self-Love in St Augustine,*. Cf. also the critique of Anders Nygren's *Agape and Eros* in Brummer, *The Model of Love*.

25 Cf. A. E. Harvey, *Promise or Pretence?* (London: SCM, 1994), p. 99.

26 McFadyen, *The Call to Personhood*, p. 161.
27 This follows from accepting Brummer's definition of love as a relationship, not just an 'attitude': cf. Brummer, *The Model of Love*.
28 *The Call to Personhood*, pp. 161, 159 (emphasis mine).
29 Alasdair MacIntyre's celebrated, if disputed, analogy in the epilogue to *After Virtue*.

9 Practices of work

1 Cf. Oliver O'Donovan, *Desire of the Nations* (Cambridge: Cambridge University Press, 1999).
2 E. Clinton Gardner, *Justice and Christian Ethics* (Cambridge: Cambridge University Press, 1995), p. 117, quoting Edmund S. Morgan, *The Puritan Dilemma: The Story of John Winthrop* (Boston: Little, Brown, 1958).
3 Gardner, *Justice and Christian Ethics*, p. 119. Gardner sees this as a broad basis for human community, better able than MacIntyre's virtue tradition to accommodate pluralism and provide a dynamic view of justice in spite of its exclusivist roots in the Judaeo-Christian tradition.
4 Peter Sedgwick, *The Market Economy and Christian Ethics* (Cambridge: Cambridge University Press, 1999); see also *The Enterprise Culture* (London: SPCK, 1992).
5 Karl Barth, *Church Dogmatics* III.4 (Edinburgh: T&T Clark, 1965); cf. Peter Sedgwick, *The Enterprise Culture*.
6 Ronald Preston, *Religion and the Ambiguities of Capitalism*, Ch. 7 (London: SCM, 1991).
7 Cf. 1 Corinthians 7.20.
8 Ronald Preston's phrase. Cf. G. Wingren, *Luther on Vocation* (Philadelphia: Muhlenberg, 1957).
9 For example, Jürgen Habermas is critical of some aspects of Weber's account of modernity and the role of work within it; this debate and its significance for identity is discussed in Sedgwick, *The Market Economy*, Ch.. 1.
10 See for example P. Lunt and S. Livingstone, *Mass Consumption and Personal Identity* (Buckingham: Open University Press, 1992).
11 Sedgwick, *The Market Economy*, especially Ch. 2: 'Consumerism and personal identity'.

12 Catherine Casey, *Work, Self and Society* (London: Routledge, 1995).

13 Charles Handy, *The Future of Work* (Oxford: Blackwell, 1984).

14 Casey, *Work, Self and Society*, p. 41.

15 Cf. Casey, *Work, Self and Society*, Ch. 2; also Flores and Gray, *Entrepreneurship and the Wired Life* (London: Demos, 2000).

16 Peter Herriot and Carole Pemberton, *New Deals. The Revolution in Managerial Careers* (Chichester: John Wiley & Sons, 1995), p. xv.

17 Handy, *The Future of Work*, p.164 (emphasis mine).

18 Cf. Richard Sennett, *The Corrosion of Character* (London and New York: Norton, 1998).

19 Flores and Gray, *Entrepreneurship*, p. 18.

20 Cf. Herriot and Pemberton, *New Deals*.

21 Casey, *Work, Self and Society*, p. 134.

22 Casey, *Work, Self and Society*, esp. pp. 149–51 and 192ff.

23 Casey, *Work, Self and Society*, p. 158.

24 Sedgwick, *The Enterprise Culture*, esp. Ch. 5.

25 The diversity of work experience is analysed by Robert Reich, *The Work of Nations* (New York: A. Knopf, 1991); cf. Sedgwick, *The Market Economy*, Ch. 3.

26 Flores and Gray, *Entrepeneurship*, p. 11 (emphasis mine).

27 Cf. D .Labier, *Modern Madness. The hidden link between work and emotional conflict* (New York: Simon and Schuster, 1986).

28 Flores and Gray, *Entrepreneurship*, p. 21.

29 Flores and Gray, *Entrepreneurship*, p. 23.

30 Flores and Gray, *Entrepreneurship*, p. 21.

31 Flores and Gray, *Entrepreneurship*, p. 26.

32 Albert O. Hirschman, *Exit, Voice, and Loyalty* (Cambridge, Mass.: Harvard University Press, 1970).

33 cf. Herriot and Pemberton, *New Deals*. Their discussion of contract makes a clear distinction between discredited forms of unilaterally imposed contract and a 'new deal' of reciprocal responsibilities and obligations which are both more binding and more flexible.

34 Reinhold Niebuhr, *Moral Man and Immoral Society* (New York: Scribners, 1932).

35 See for example G. Chryssides and J. Kaler, *Essentials of*

Business Ethics (London: McGraw Hill, 1996); Roger Bradburn, *Understanding Business Ethics* (London: Continuum, 2001).

36 For example, M. L. Nieto cites evidence from work with the Virgin group, that 'successful commercial performance was achievable when profits were placed in third place of importance, below staff and customers' ('Business ethics for the twenty-first century': paper delivered at the Business Ethics Conference, University of Surrey, 6 March 2002).

37 Cf. Herriot and Pemberton, *New Deals*. This includes some discussion of the practical possibilities of transmitting the continuous *worth* of the worker across different activities both within and outside the organization.

38 Flores and Gray begin to explore this in *Entrepreneurship*.

39 Bradburn notes how the rotation of staff which 'frustrated stable working relationships' was identified as a contributory factor in corporate responsibility for the *Herald of Free Enterprise* disaster of 1987: *Understanding Business Ethics*, p. 177.

40 Cf. Hirschman, *Exit, Voice, and Loyalty*, p. 101.

41 Cf. Herriot and Pemberton, *New Deals*, where this need is recognized and some possibilties of putting it into practice are discussed.

42 Bradburn, *Understanding Business Ethics*, p. 182.

43 See Flores and Gray, *Entrepreneurship*. Cf. also Charles Handy, *The Age of Paradox* (Boston: Harvard Business School Press, 1994).

44 For example, M. Douglas Meeks, *God the Economist: The doctrine of God and political economy* (Minneapolis: Fortress Press, 1989). Cited especially by Sedgwick.

Conclusion: Time, change, identity: the call to faithfulness

1 Edward Thomas, *Collected Poems* (Oxford: Oxford University Press, 1981).

INDEX OF SUBJECTS

INDEX OF NAMES